# THE PSYCHIC HEALING BOOK

# THE PSYCHIC HEALING BOOK

AMY WALLACE
AND BILL HENKIN

*Wingbow Press/Berkeley*

Wingbow Press books are published
and distributed by Bookpeople,
2929 Fifth St., Berkeley, CA 94710

Excerpt from LIFE AFTER LIFE by Raymond Moody, M.D.,
(Bantam Books, 1975) used by permission of
Mockingbird Books, Inc.

Cover design by Michael Patrick Cronan

Designed by Oksana Kushnir

First Wingbow printing: October, 1981
Second printing: August, 1983
Third printing: January, 1985

## Acknowledgments

This book has been written by two people. Yet, in a sense, I feel it has been written by many. Through the years I've received personal and professional support and assistance from many, many people—some of whom never knew they were my teachers and guides, most of whom wouldn't have cared if they knew. A few of these people have been overtly concerned with my development, and I would like to acknowledge them for their support and assistance, and for sharing in the adventure that is my life and my road. With love, and thanks for services rendered: Lewis Bostwick, Ken Burke, Bob Byars, Evelyn Chaitkin, Dennis Conkin, Ann Crawford, Niki Henkin, Carl Levett, Mark Malkas, Pam Neal, Grace Shapiro, Rachel Jack Thompson, Amy Wallace, and especially Werner Erhard and Diane Nelson.

BILL HENKIN

For their help in writing this book and enjoying my life and all that stuff, I would like to thank: Dennis, Lewis, Mark Rothe, Helen Palmer, John Bean, Mark Malkas, Amelie, Tamara, Bill, David and Flora, and special thanks to Mom and Dad. XXX.

AMY WALLACE

Miracles are natural. When they do not occur, something has gone wrong.

—A Course in Miracles

# CONTENTS

*Contents*

## Contents

THE
PSYCHIC
HEALING
BOOK

# INTRODUCTION

This is not a book about miracles. It is a book about you, your life, and the lives of the people around you. It is a book about all of us: about the powers we all have, usually without even realizing it. It is about honesty and communication, with ourselves and with others. It is as much a book about *being* well as it is a book about *getting* well.

There are many psychic books. Most of them fall into one of two categories—"spiritual" psychic books, advocating that the reader adopt a certain set of religious beliefs if he or she wishes to experience the psychic world, and books written by parapsychologists and other scientists *about* psychics, studying their powers. While these books are valuable contributions to the field, they often make dry reading.

This is a different kind of book—a psychic "how-to"

book. It is unique because the concept behind it is unique: that *everyone* is psychic, and everyone can develop natural psychic skills in his or her own life, without crystal balls, Tarot cards, or black cats.

It is our perception that psychic skills are not magical, accidental "gifts" which only a few people possess. Rather, every person has these skills and can develop them if they want to.

Psychic healing is a phenomenon at least as old as recorded history. It has been a popular subject for medical scientists and humanistic philosophers for centuries. It has also been through some hard times, times when it was out of favor with the general public.

We live in a period when people are coming to recognize and enjoy their natural psychic abilities. The problem is that our culture still accepts the notion that everyone's natural abilities—to be psychic, and to heal themselves—are secret, esoteric, and can only be mastered after years of dedicated study.

Part of the purpose of this book is to demonstrate that this notion is not necessarily so. While everyone possesses these natural abilities, we've noticed that most people have not allowed themselves the freedom of working with these powers because they were afraid of them, or because they believed that they didn't have enough background, intelligence, sensitivity, or whatever to learn to use them. To this we say, "Nonsense."

Psychic abilities, and healing abilities, are your natural birthright. It does not require secret passwords or years of labor in some Himalayan cave in order to activate them and use them in your life. Indeed, you are probably using them already, although you may not be aware of it.

This book is a combination of practical techniques and

2

a discussion of different facets of the psychic world. You may practice all these techniques either by yourself or with friends. It is best to read each exercise thoroughly before you begin it. Or, you may have a friend read it to you step by step as you go along. Or, you may leave the book lying open beside you as you work, and refer to it as you come to each new step.

Psychic stuff is not "spooky" as it is so often thought to be. Nor, however, is it a party game. We trust that using your psychic skills will enrich your daily life in a deep and meaningful way and will open up new avenues of adventure for you.

Throughout the book we will be mentioning specific incidents in our own lives that seem to us to illustrate particular points we want to make. Some of these incidents happened in Amy's life and some in Bill's. A few of them happened in both of our lives, either separately and at different times, or, occasionally, to both of us at once. Since you are going to be getting to know us through the book, we'd like to take a few pages here to let you know what our psychic lives are like and how it was that we came to discover and work with our own psychic abilities.

## Amy's Story

People are constantly asking me, "How did you get into this? When did you know that you were psychic? Did you have a powerful psychic experience that led you to believe you had this gift?"

The answers to these questions are fairly mundane. I stumbled into psychic studies by having a psychic reading.

Before that I had never had a grand psychic experience that caused me to feel that I had a special gift. Rather, a sense of my own psychic specialness grew slowly—the really exciting things began to happen after I was a couple of years into it.

When I was fifteen, I became interested in unusual forms of healing, such as herbal medicine, acupuncture, nutrition, etc., all of which I have dabbled in. My friends flocked to me with their head colds and stomachaches, and my potions seemed to work wonders. I decided to pursue the field of healing, but I had no particular interest in psychic healing.

When I was eighteen, I moved to Berkeley, California. A friend of mine had a friend who claimed to be "psychic"— on a whim I decided to have a reading. I don't know what I expected exactly, except I secretly hoped my reader would tell me what a great psychic I was. He didn't do that at all. Instead he concentrated on my relationships with my family and friends, pointing out to me why some of these relationships were unsuccessful and what I could do about it.

I was so intrigued with the whole process that I decided to find out where this psychic had learned his stuff. He directed me to the Berkeley Psychic Institute, a school run by Lewis Bostwick. At the time, it had twenty or so full-time students. Lewis had traveled widely; he had been involved with a number of religions and mystical traditions and had culled his own philosophy and method of teaching from them. The school advertised by word of mouth, and people came from all over for readings and healings. The full-time course at the Institute consists of a combination of lecture/meditations led by Lewis, and sitting next to more experienced psychic readers daily and observing their

4

methods. Eventually, the beginning students began to do simple readings on their own, and so on from there. The school also offers basic courses in healing with spirit guides.

I progressed rapidly at the Institute, and in no time I was seeing auras and giving healings. My first dramatic healing was making a headache disappear at a party. Since then, I have helped people with much more dramatic ailments heal themselves. Here are a few:

1. Martha, a twenty-two-year-old woman, had scarred fallopian tubes and was supposedly sterile. Doctors told her she would never have another child. After several healings, she returned to one of these doctors, who discovered that the scar tissue had disappeared. She now has a child.

2. Sam, in his forties, had, years before meeting me, suffered partial paralysis from which he had considerably recovered, although he still suffered from painful muscle spasms and severe depression. He had tried chiropractic, acupuncture, and traditional allopathic treatment to allay his pain. After several healings, his muscle spasms ceased, and his depression lifted.

3. Marie, thirty-three, had abnormal vaginal bleeding, which had continued for several weeks. The bleeding stopped after a healing.

4. Alice, in her twenties, had severe colitis and was largely bedridden. After a few healings, her painful attacks ceased, and she was up and around.

5. Patricia, a three-week-old premature baby, was born with an open heart valve. She was close to death when she received a long-distance healing, and her heart valve began to close in a matter of hours. She is now a healthy baby.

6. Anna, a woman in her mid-forties, had arthritis of the neck and right knee. It disappeared entirely after one heal-

ing. A year later arthritis developed in her left hip. It was again completely cured after one healing.

I have also helped people to partial recovery in cases of hemophilia, multiple sclerosis, cancer, arthritis, and spinal disorders.

After about a year, I decided it was time to leave the Institute and go off on my own. I began to teach classes in developing psychic skills to groups and individuals. I also began giving readings and healings in my home, and I still do.

Around this time, a friend of mine from the Institute began developing trance mediumship. He learned to leave his physical body and let a spirit enter and speak through it. I had seen this ability demonstrated a few times at the Institute but was astonished to find that one of my friends possessed it. The beings who spoke through him were more than kind, and we began a course of study with them. They lectured (through my friend) on various psychic phenomena and instructed us in more advanced meditations than we had learned at the school. We continued in this way for about a year, until my friend left Berkeley.

Needless to say, these two years had quite an effect on my own personal life. A lot of my friends thought the things I was doing were weird. And to make it worse, I went through a period of being pushy about psychic stuff. I thought it was the greatest thing in the world: It had upped my enthusiasm for living enormously, it was lots of fun, I was meeting new and exciting people, and I had found an independent way to make a living. And I thought everyone I knew should do exactly what I was doing. I only wanted to know people who were "psychic." I guess you could say I was a psychic snob.

After a couple of years and some unpleasant experiences,

this psychic chauvinism wore off. I realized that I *didn't* want all my friends to do what I was doing—to be around professional psychics all the time can be as boring as being around professional anything-elses all the time. What's more, I had made an even more important discovery: I really didn't want to be "psychic" all the time.

As we will demonstrate, you can't read anyone's mind or peek at his aura unless he wants you to. Now, I've never been much for mind-reading, but for a long time I was not above aura-peeking. It made me feel superior. But, eventually, the thrill wore off. After a long day of giving readings, I want my time *off.* Sometimes I don't want to think, talk, or act psychic until my next reading or healing. Many people, however, are no more respectful of a psychic's time off than they are of a doctor's—we have all seen people bothering doctors, lawyers, plumbers, etc., for their professional advice at a party. People expect me to read their auras and see their futures at parties, on the telephone, anywhere. In general, I tell people that I can counsel them by appointment only.

Despite these inconveniences, the benefits I've derived from being psychic are enormous. There is one in particular I would like to mention. If I had one strong psychic ability throughout my life, it was an extremely acute awareness of other people's feelings. I could always sense what other people were feeling, except that I often could not tell these feelings from my own. I have now developed a sense of my own boundaries, of where my feelings let off and another person's begin. I can observe another person's feelings compassionately, without necessarily getting caught up in his or her suffering. Every time I do a healing, I am giving myself a little reminder of this, and these reminders are of inestimable value to me.

Just because I am psychic, my life has by no means become a bowl of cherries. I am continually bumping into the same problems and difficulties as everyone else, and getting just as frustrated by them. However, my frustrations have become much less extreme. This is because I have an increasing sense that I am not a victim of circumstance, but that my life is my own very exciting, infinitely beautiful creation.

## Bill's Story

Since I was a child I've felt an affinity for those psychic perceptions we know as ESP—the ability to know something I had no apparent way of knowing. And as I grew up, this affinity became stronger. It was particularly pronounced during the years I was in college; when the phone would ring, I would *know* that the call was for me, and who was on the other end—sometimes even before the phone actually rang. It happened in other areas as well: Now and then I'd walk into a room where some music was playing and know who the composer was, even if I'd never heard the music before. Once I wrote a college exam—and passed —on a book I'd never read, simply because the information was just *there* for me. Sometimes when I write I don't even think about what I'm going to say. Like the answers to the exam, the information is just *there*.

After I moved to California, I found that a number of my friends were pursuing psychic activities quite actively. One woman who had emphysema experienced a spontaneous remission after attending a healers' convention. Others were able to read auras. I was impressed, but upset, because I couldn't even meditate: My mind would always wander and settle on the most exasperating things that were going on in my life at the moment, or that had gone on in the past, or might go on in the future. On the few occasions when I got into a nice, smooth trance, my tranquillity would vanish as soon as I opened my eyes. Although I *knew* that I had psychic abilities, I couldn't seem to harness them at all. It was an extremely frustrating period for me.

In 1974 I spent the summer in Katonah, New York, editing and producing a book on transpersonal psychology. I spent fourteen weeks in the company of several people who had been working conscientiously to liberate themselves from their personal prisons through meditative disciplines. I could see that these people knew something about something that I didn't know about, and wanted to. With their assistance, I began to meditate, pay attention to my actions and the chatter that was always going on in the back of my mind, and to read books by and about people who had had various forms of psychic experience.

I returned to California on a Thursday. On Friday I began to study at the Berkeley Psychic Institute. A few months later I began to work with a Jungian Buddhist psychologist whose approach to our work supported my psychic development. All through this time I was keeping dream journals and reading a potpourri of classic mystic texts and contemporary popular self-help books which were signposts on my jungle-tangled road.

Late the following summer I took the *est* training, which created, for me, a context in which everything I had been studying began to fall into place. The people I met in the *est* organization didn't find psychic abilities unusual—they seemed to me to just *assume* them, and to go on from there.

It was okay with them if I was psychic, and what about my *life?* It was perfect support.

As I continued my studies, I found that the "energies" that we will discuss in this book were more and more available to me, that I didn't have to *do* anything to make them available: They were just there, waiting for me, the way the answers to that college exam were. And then, over the course of a few months, I began to notice that my life was a lot more enjoyable than it ever had been. The bad times became almost pleasant, and the good times were filled with an ineffable rapture.

One evening I was sitting home writing poetry when I realized that everything in my life was exactly the way I wanted it to be. I was doing what I wanted to be doing, I had what I wanted to have, and I was who I wanted to be. I had an experience of total satisfaction with my life. A few months after this incident, I was again sitting home writing poetry. This time, however, I realized that nothing in my life was as I wanted it to be: I was not being who I wanted to be, I was not doing what I wanted to do, and I did not have what I wanted to have. And again, I had an experience of total satisfaction with my life—even though it looked to me as if nothing in my life was working out.

I have no idea what these experiences mean, except that for the first time in my life I felt free. I don't mean "free" in any nihilistic sense—not free-floating, not free of the world or my place in it. Rather, free to float or not to float; free to be myself instead of who I thought I was supposed to be, or who other people thought I was supposed to be. And by free, I also do not mean unattached, uncommitted, or that I had no problems. Not at all. I still had all the problems I had before, I was still attached to things—material, spiritual, and so on—and I was still committed to people, to what I wanted to do in the world, and to many of my pictures. But I had begun to dislodge some of the frantic needs to be a certain way, do something, or have something that had often, in the past, driven me to a fury of despair or an impotent rage. I began to be free just to be.

In my newfound state the good times and bad times occur within a framework that is, relatively, beyond good or bad; in a sense, beyond my concern. While in one sense nothing in my life has changed at all, in another sense I really don't see that it matters how I feel, or what I think: It's all just fine the way it is. And there I find the energies again, existing themselves in a state both in the world and out of the world. I find that all I have to do to use the energies is to know very clearly what I want, and get out of the way so it can happen. Sometimes I'm successful and sometimes not. Sometimes I surprise myself, forgetting that these energies are real, and then having, for instance, some ridiculous wish come true. Sometimes what I wish for is *not* what I want! And sometimes what I want is not what I wish for.

Unlike Amy, I am not a practicing professional healer. I have studied healing, along with other areas of psychic development, and I have performed, individually or working with other psychics, perhaps a hundred healings, ranging from headaches and warts to cancer and hepatitis. Sometimes these healings succeed, sometimes they fail and sometimes they are partially successful.

I enjoy working as a healer both because I like people to feel good, and because it is work that makes me feel good. When I heal another, I am cleansed and healed in the process. But my principal interest in psychic healing is that it is a road out of a kind of forest of cosmic ignorance into the sunlight of personal realization. I have found psychic

11

healing to be a road—not *the* road—of liberation. And from time to time I find that I can assist others along their own roads through what I have discovered for myself.

In a sense, writing this book has been a process of psychic healing for me. As, perhaps, reading it will be a psychic healing process for you. It's been a kind of life-exercise in which I have had the opportunity to examine my work and thoughts, my experiences and observations, and to offer some of them for use in your life. Along the way, I have grown tremendously, and my own abilities have become clearer and more focused. Perhaps something like that will happen for you. But whatever happens as you read this book, enjoy yourself, and let us know how you like *The Psychic Healing Book*.

You can write to us, Amy Wallace or Bill Henkin, P.O. Box 4501, Berkeley, California 94704.

# 1

# WE ARE
# ALL PSYCHIC

### What Is Being "Psychic"?

The telephone rings and, although you haven't heard from her or thought of her in months, you say, "That must be Aunt Margie." And it is.

You turn on the television set to watch a football game. Somehow, in a sudden flash, without even thinking about it, you know which team is going to win. And it does.

You go to a party and meet someone you've never met before, yet you're certain you know him from someplace.

We've all had these kinds of experiences which we sloughed off as coincidence, or explained away with some pseudo-scientific reasoning, or simply called good luck. Yet, over the course of our lives, they keep happening, leaving us with a sense that we've occasionally stepped across some invisible boundary into mysterious realms, where miracles occur as a matter of course, and where we are as gods, knowing what we as ordinary mortals cannot possibly know.

These are the realms of the psychic, and contrary to popular tradition, they are not reserved for pasty-faced dandies with ascots and velvet jackets, or for half-senile ex-captains of the British navy, or for dowdy spinsters who live with eighteen cats in dimly lit rooming houses. They are realms of our own reality which we ignore because we are frightened, or because we've been told since we were infants that they don't exist, or because we don't understand them and don't understand how they relate to our everyday lives. But if we watch ourselves as we make our daily rounds, we see how often we participate in them and how much of our lives we govern by the things we know and yet couldn't know.

The great Greek philosopher Plato noted that all learning is just the soul's remembering. There will be a good deal of talk in this book about the "soul," or the "spirit," or the "being," or the "entity." These are all terms that designate that part of each of us that has its existence on some other plane of being than the physical, material one we know so well.

We don't know exactly what your image of the "soul" is, or whether you even think such a thing exists. When we use the word we mean that part of each of us which seems to know things we know we cannot know. We mean the part of us that feels genuine love for all other beings and lets us feel, now and then, that it really is more blessed to give than to receive, simply for the joy of serving another. We mean that part of each of us which survives—if anything does—after our bodies, minds, emotions, and intellects die.

14

We say, "if anything does," because we really don't *know* that anything survives our bodies except other people's memories of us. But we talk about the "soul" or the "spirit" as if it had this capability because on the one hand it explains a lot that is otherwise inexplicable, and on the other hand because as we delve further and further into the realms of the so-called psychic, we come more and more in contact with our own versions of the experiences discussed by all the great mystics and prophets, from Jesus Christ and Gautama Buddha to Uri Geller and Edgar Cayce.

## What Is Being a Psychic Healer?

Psychic abilities and healing abilities are so closely related that there's almost no point in making any distinction between them. Healers are people who have learned to direct their psychic skills in the particular direction of alleviating physical pain and suffering. But just as we sometimes know who is on the other end of the phone before we answer it, so we also know how to heal ourselves and others. We just don't pay much attention to these abilities because we believe that we don't have them, or because we fear them.

It is a truism of psychology that we fear most the things we understand least. It is partly the purpose of this book to make these misunderstood realms comprehensible to you. It is our hope and expectation that the more familiar you become with them, and the more you understand them in terms of your own life, the less mysterious they will be and, therefore, the more access you will have to the abilities you already possess. Examine your own experience of that one great mystery—your life—and see if what we say is borne out there. If what we say is not true for you in your own experience it is, in the realest sense, not true.


## Animism and Spiritism

The word "psychic" derives from the Greek word *psychikos,* which means "of the soul," or "spiritual" (from the Greek *psychē,* which means "the soul," or "spirit"). It refers to that which is beyond natural or known physical processes. It also refers to a person who is sensitive to forces beyond the physical world. A psychic healer, then, is a person who utilizes his or her sensitivity to such forces in the process of curing physical hurts.

Two great theories predominate in the history of psychic healing. They are known as the *animist* and the *spiritist* theories. The first theory holds that all psychic powers lie within the soul of the individual, although in most people they are undeveloped and largely unused. The second theory assumes the existence of disembodied spirits who talk or work through living people known as *mediums.* Just as we cannot demonstrate the existence of the soul in the way we can demonstrate, for instance, an ice-cream cone, so also we cannot demonstrate the existence of discorporate entities, or "spirits." But as with other intangible aspects of psychism, the fact that we cannot hold spirits in our hand does not mean they don't exist.

In a sense, it doesn't matter which of these theories is more attractive to you. If it seems to you that your psychic abilities are your own, then you will call them up from your deeper consciousness at your own pace and to serve your own needs. If it seems to you that spirits work through you, or that angels guide your steps, then you will call on these other beings for information and assistance. In either case you will work from those levels of your deeper self that we know as the psychic realm.

Our own prejudice favors the animist theory, since it is one step closer to ourselves than spiritism is, and since it is therefore easier to see the ways in which we are each, finally and fundamentally, the creators of our own experiences. But in either case the processes of getting in touch with your psychic abilities are essentially the same, and from time to time in this book it may seem as if the theories overlap. The work is all the same, the discoveries are the same, and the use to which you can put your knowledge is the same. We are always talking about your psychic world.

One of the basic tenets of this book is that everything in life, in the world, and in the cosmos is unfolding exactly as it is supposed to, whether we realize it at any given moment or not. This doesn't mean that we should crawl into bed and wait for whatever's going to happen to happen. It doesn't mean that we shouldn't live our lives fully, enthusiastically, and ethically. It doesn't mean that we don't have choice, at every moment, about how we will live, or how we will experience ourselves and our lives and those of the people around us. It means simply that we have the freedom to view and live our lives in any way that gives us the most satisfaction—the sincerest and deepest pleasure.

Christ advised that we should render unto Caesar what is Caesar's, and unto God what is God's. The world of the psychic is a dichotomous world, where God and Caesar both get their due. You pay taxes, not because you like to pay taxes but because taxes are there to be paid. You experience your deeper self, or God, or you become a healer, not because it will make you a better person, or even a happier one, necessarily, but because it's there.

## Being at One

No matter what religious or philosophical background you have, you have probably heard the idea that *we are all one,* or even that *all is one.* There is a state of being—or, if you prefer, a level of consciousness—in which this idea ceases to be mere words and becomes real because you experience the truth of it. Perhaps you are already familiar with this state. It becomes clear for many people in the experience of love, when we feel our very soul merge with that of another. Sometimes when we work with a group of people toward some common goal we have a similar experience of unity, or of being related to everyone else in the group. It is but a short step from love for another, or for a group of others, to the powerful and supposedly mystical experience of loving and merging with everyone, or even with everything.

The state of being at one is something all the saints and sages in recorded history refer to. Until we have the experience ourselves, many of us resist it, or avoid it, or fear it because we think that in having the experience we will lose touch with our own individuality. Nothing could be further from the truth. Indeed, it is in the mystical state of oneness that we most completely experience who we truly are. It is there, more than in any other state of consciousness, that we most thoroughly become ourselves, because there is no way to have the total experience of unity with others with-

18

out first having a total experience of unity with self. When have you been more yourself than when you loved another? When have you been more yourself in a group than when you loved the group and felt a oneness with it?

As you proceed in this book you will find some simple exercises which will lead you in the direction of having these kinds of experiences. The exercises are arranged to allow you to move through them one step at a time. You need never go on from one exercise to the next until you feel ready to do so; and you can benefit from reading beyond the exercise you're working on, even though you don't feel ready to undertake the more complicated exercises. Although it may not look that way right now, you're not going to learn anything from this book, except techniques, that you don't already know. You *are* going to learn that you already know something you may think, right now, you don't know.

One of the first steps in doing healings is finding your spiritual center, and learning to love yourself and others from there, instead of from the hotbed of your needs and desires. To the degree your love comes from such a place, you can perceive that all things are related and that they are actually part of the same, larger, one.

When all is one, you are freed from the necessity of passing judgment on particular things. This is the state "beyond good and evil," in which nothing is right or wrong, good or bad, better or worse. When you are an observer in the state of oneness, you are totally psychic.

At the point of receiving information psychically, you can move in the direction of healing with very little extra effort. When you want to heal a friend of yours, you enter into a state of oneness with him or her, and then ask *yourself* about your friend's physical condition. Since your friend is, at this point, another part of you, you find you already know the answers. And on the basis of the answers you get from yourself, you can begin to do healing work on your friend.

As the preceding few paragraphs indicate, there is a step between being at one with yourself and others, and healing. That step, in which you receive information, is known to psychics as "reading." A psychic reading may take any of a number of forms, but in some way it always precedes, and is part of, a healing.

## The Astral Body

Just as you have a physical anatomy, you also possess a psychic anatomy, which consists principally of the aura— those emanations of energy that surround all living things —and the chakras (pronounced SHOCK-rahs)—specific energy points in the aura. This nonphysical anatomy is known as the "astral body" and is capable of leaving the physical body for periods of time. This state is known as "astral travel." We will discuss astral travel as it pertains to healings in Chapter 8, MORE ADVANCED HEALING AND READING TECHNIQUES.

## Auras and Colors

The aura does not only exist in the imagination. It has been photographed by the Kirlian process in rigidly controlled scientific experiments. Psychics use aura readings to determine the health, and the mental, emotional, and psychic conditions of their clients. Psychics often see auras in color, but sometimes the aura will appear, instead, in the form of waves or other energy patterns. Some psychics do not even see the aura but receive an impression of what the aura would look like if they could see it. And others simply get a sense of the energy surrounding a person, which doesn't translate into visual terms at all.

Although visualization techniques, which we will discuss in some detail as this book progresses, are extremely useful tools, they are just tools, and no single tool is indispensable in psychic work. Each tool is a source of assistance to you, to use or not use as the situation and your own inclination dictate.

Different traditions detail as many as seven separate auric layers, but for our purposes we need deal with only one aura. In our own work we find that all the information we need as readers and healers is contained in this aura.

The healthy aura extends about one foot from the body, from head to toe. As it happens, a great many people are walking around without whole auras. For example, if you are a sedentary person who rarely takes walks or exercise, you are likely to have a thin, wispy aura below the knees. Or, if you have an injured part of your body, or are otherwise estranged from it because you think it unattractive or unhealthy, your aura will probably be weak in that area.

As we've mentioned, the aura is not always seen in color. Many beginning readers see it as a wavy, flowing, whitish band. However, for the purpose of reading, many psychics flip a switch, so to speak, on their mental TV screens so that they can see the aura in a variety of shifting colors, and use the differences to interpret a client's condition.

While it is possible, in the most general way, to ascribe

specific meanings to different colors and patterns, colors are seen in a highly subjective light, and no two readers will see precisely the same shades in any aura at any given time. If you wish to give psychic readings—for fun or profit—it will be useful to come to a sense of what colors mean to you in general. But it is rather more important to be able to see each color freshly every time, as if you had never seen it before, and to discover anew what the color means in its particular context each time it appears. Auras are in a state of constant flux. Their colors and patterns shift with each passing thought or feeling. In addition, the colors blend and merge as they fluctuate, and, as in a rainbow, it is often impossible to say exactly where one color leaves off and the next begins.

We really urge you to do all your reading as if you were discovering the entire process for the first time each time you read. Yet, we are aware that your task will be easier, and your learning clearer, if you have some idea of what it is you're looking for. The following list is intended to be a guide for you, but allow it to be modified by your own experience.

In the most general sense, colors may be read as follows:

*Black*     Black is the color of death and destruction, and may be read as a sign of depression—particularly when it appears as a dark cloud hovering over a person's head. However, death is the state that precedes rebirth, and destruction is the state that precedes construction, or creativity. "The darkest hour comes just before the dawn." In this sense, black can be seen as an extremely positive color. Black is also seen as representing the invisible light of God, come to pierce and purify the soul.

*Gray*     Gray is the color of boredom and malaise, usually masking emotions of fear or anger.

*Brown*    Ordinarily brown is an Earth color and indicates a strong connection with the physical plane. When it shows up around the feet and legs, it may indicate that the person gets a lot of exercise. Sometimes—particularly if the color is dull and washed-out—it may be a sign of low energy.

*Green*    Green is a growth color whose presence in the aura usually indicates that a person is undergoing change in his attitudes, beliefs, or way of life. It is a positive color which may show up when a person, under the stresses of major internal change, thinks his life is going badly. Light apple green is a sign of psychic development.

*Blue*    Blue is the color of creativity, imagination, and self-expression. Like the sea and sky, which are among its symbols, it indicates a feminine nature, or the feminine side of a masculine nature. Dark blue is often a sign of repression, which develops when a person acts on other people's ideas of who he is or how he should behave, rather than on his own.

*Yellow*    Yellow, the color of the intellect, represents the process of changing the unconscious to conscious. It suggests changes and moves of all sorts, especially those that lead toward refinement and the growth of the mind. Yellow is most often seen as a halo around the head.

*Orange*    Orange is primarily a healing color. Like the sun, which is one of its symbols, it indicates a masculine nature, or the masculine side of a feminine nature. When seen in the aura it may mean the person possesses strong healing abilities, or it may mean he is in the process of healing himself physically or emotionally.

*Pink*    Pink is a color of intuition and instinctive knowledge about the Earth. It is sometimes called the color of "planetary intuition."

*Red*    Red is the color of the emotions and of warming to life. Strong feelings of any kind, such as anger, fear, or love, are represented by red. Dark red is likely to indicate repressed, troubling emotions, while a bright, clean red signifies intensity and passion.

*Purple*    Purple is the color of spirituality and devotion. People who meditate or have strong religious feelings usually display this color in their auras.

*Gold*    Gold is the color of pure intuition, psychic prowess, and self-knowledge. Mystics and other people in states of bliss are often seen sporting radiant golden halos. Gold is a masculine color, often represented by the sun. It is also a cleansing and healing color.

*Silver*    Silver, the feminine color of the moon, is similar in meaning to gold, though seen less often. A great deal of silver in the aura may indicate prowess in such psychic feats as telekinesis (bending or moving objects by thought) or levitation. Silver is the color of astral travel, and it is said that a silver cord attaches the astral body to the physical body when the two are apart.

*White*    Pure white is the color of the highest spiritual attainment, purification, and enlightenment. However, certain types of meditation, such as TM, which may or may not produce enlightenment, can produce this color in the aura.

Auras are read like maps, and colors frequently appear in relation to one another. Thus, for instance, you may see a dark red around the heart, and you may read this red as anger arising from someone's being hurt emotionally. Orange next to the red, then, might mean that the person is in the process of healing his wound, since orange is a healing color. If, in the same aura, you see green (a growth color) mingled with yellow (the color of the intellect) around the head, you might conclude that out of his pain this person is discovering new ways to think about things and changing his old mental patterns.

The colors in an aura can appear to be evenly layered, like a layer cake; they can be blotchy and chaotic; or they can be mixed together in a muddy mess. Whatever its color scheme, it is rare to see an aura which is not in flux, glowing and changing to reflect the shifting moods of the person. While this may make the process of aura reading sound difficult, it is the delicate and subtle shifts of consciousness and states of mind which change most rapidly. The general, prominent colors in an aura change more slowly, over a period of weeks, months, and even years.

Shapes, like colors, are subject to the reader's interpretation and to the particular energy of the other person. For example, waves that emanate out from the body may indicate strength and charisma—the "glow" we feel coming from some particularly powerful people—but they may also indicate an absence of attachment to the physical plane, which prevents a person from fulfilling himself completely.

## The Chakras

Psychics also read the colors and shapes in an aura in relation to the chakras, which are energy points distributed throughout the astral body. In Hindu cosmology, an individual's chakra development indicates his state of psychic development. The word *chakra* means "wheel" in Sanskrit, and Indian yogis see the chakras as small, dully colored disks, usually about the size of a silver dollar, in the astral bodies of psychically undeveloped people. As a person becomes fully awakened, his chakras open and whirl like brightly colored flowers.

There are many approaches to reading chakras. Cabalistic readers identify ten separate energy points. An American scientist has drawn a relationship between the chakras and the glands of the endocrine system. Tibetan readers read as a single chakra what we regard as two separate chakras (the sixth and seventh). And in some philosophical systems, including those which underlie this book, the chakras are read as indicators of a person's general state of being, including his health and his preparedness to undertake whatever tasks he has set for himself in this lifetime.

Although we identify the chakras as they correspond to parts of the physical body, they do not exist there in any sense. They appear in the astral body and are located in terms of the physical body for convenience, both in reading and healing. Energy directed toward a particular chakra in the astral body will act on that part of the physical body as well.

For our purposes we identify and work with seven principal chakras and four secondary ones. All eleven energy centers are connected to an "energy channel" which runs behind and parallel with the spine. The chakras can be opened or closed at will, for the purpose of encouraging or discouraging different psychic abilities, and we will offer techniques for manipulating the chakras in Chapter 3, SELF-HEALING.

A chakra can become damaged and may then appear to the reader to be cracked. A chakra can also tilt out of alignment with the energy channel. Such chakral disorders are generally caused by psychological stress or trauma. Such stress or trauma may be brought on by events or feelings which we regard as "positive" as well as by those we regard as "negative." Anything which disturbs an individual's normal functioning has the potential to disturb the chakras as well. For example, very often the memory of a painful event (which can be seen clairvoyantly as a literal image, which we call a "picture" or an "image") will become lodged in a chakra and distort or obstruct the flow of energy to or from that chakra. Physical as well as psychological problems can result from these blockages, and a healer can frequently accomplish a great deal simply by cleaning out and aligning the chakras—a technique we will discuss in Chapter 5, SOME ADVANCED HEALING AND READING TECHNIQUES.

The first, or "root," chakra is located at the base of the spine in men, and between the ovaries in women. It is the only chakra whose location is sex-differentiated. It is sometimes called the "survival" chakra, and is concerned with those mechanisms which keep the physical body alive. For instance, when you are in immediate danger, or in any emergency situation, your first chakra will open up and release the store of information you need to stay alive, or to help someone else stay alive. If you're out of money, out of a job, and you just got evicted from your apartment, the chances are pretty good that you're "in survival," or "in your first chakra." This is to say that most or all of your psychic attention is being directed to maintaining the basics of life.

The second, or "spleen," chakra is located just below the navel. It is the energy center through which we perceive other people's emotions. The psychic ability to feel how other people are feeling is called *clairsentience* (clear knowing). Many people have active second chakras and are psychic in this way without realizing it. A little bit of clairsentience is a good thing because it allows you to be sensitive to other people and to sense dangerous situations. But having a wide-open second chakra can be traumatic. A common problem arising from a wide-open second chakra may develop something like this: You're in a good mood when you meet your friend for coffee and a chat, but your friend has problems and is depressed. You're sympathetic and understanding, and help your friend to see the bright side of his situation. Feeling much better, your friend goes away happy and relieved. You, on the other hand, feel strangely depressed. Without knowing it, you've taken on your friend's problems and feelings.

We discourage cultivating clairsentience as a psychic ability because there are less complicated, less trouble-producing ways to be psychic.

The second chakra is also concerned with sexual energy and is the point from which we send and receive sexual feelings. It is an important center in the practice of tantric yoga, which is a type of meditation focusing on sexual union as a way of achieving higher states of consciousness.

The third chakra, located at the solar plexus, is the body's distribution point for psychic energies—a sort of psychic energy pump. Although it is located somewhat higher than the navel, it is the chakra in question when you "contemplate your navel." A third chakra operating improperly will adversely affect all the psychic energies in the body and create a general imbalance and disharmony in a person. When you're frightened or nervous, and your stomach clenches up, you are feeling the tightening of this center.

The fourth chakra, located at the heart, is the chakra of love, affinity, and compassion. It is the chakra of oneness which operates in true self-love (different from narcissism), love for another, love for a group, or love for all and everything. Many types of Eastern meditation center on the opening of the fourth chakra.

The fifth chakra, located at the throat, at the base of the larynx, is the chakra of communication. If you have something to say and you're not saying it, your throat chakra will tighten up and result in a sore throat, laryngitis, or "a frog in your throat." If you're particularly sensitive, you'll feel a response in your own fifth chakra when someone else has something pressing to tell you. A closed, or partially closed, fifth chakra is a practically universal ailment, and is the bane of many a psychic reader and healer.

Group telepathy is also associated with the fifth chakra, as is *clairaudience* (clear hearing), which is hearing voices psychically. Most importantly, this is the center through which you receive your "inner voice," that part of you which is the real you, and which always gives you the right advice. Another way of saying this is that the fifth chakra is where your spirit, or soul (which always knows what's good for you), communicates with your mind, or personality (which usually needs a little coaching).

The sixth chakra, located in the center of the forehead, is the "third eye." It is the chakra of visualization, which enables you to see auras, chakras (your own and other people's), and pictures in your head. The ability to visualize is called *clairvoyance* (clear seeing) and is used to varying degrees by the majority of psychic readers. A clogged sixth chakra will often result in a headache.

Another function of this center is to let you know when other people are thinking of you, which is a form of "mental telepathy." When someone directs a strong flow of energy toward you, either because he's wondering what's on your mind or because he has you on his mind, he is "in your head." You may perceive this condition as a dull ache—

usually more like pressure than like pain—just above and between your eyebrows.

The opening of the third eye is considered to be a major event in many mystical traditions, as a representation of spiritual awakening and enlightenment. However, it is not necessary to develop this center in order to be psychic.

The seventh, or "crown," chakra is located at the top of the head. This is the chakra of "knowingness," or pure intuition. When a psychic goes into trance, he brings cosmic energy into his body through this chakra, and directs it throughout his other centers. Cosmic energy is, of course, the energy of the cosmos. It has a direct correspondence to the energy of the Earth, known as Earth energy. Proper utilization of each of these energies, and of a combination of the two, not only provides a healer with a certain psychic stability but also assists him in becoming and remaining a "clear channel" when reading and healing. We will discuss a technique for taking in and applying these energies in Chapter 3, SELF-HEALING. When the seventh chakra is open and properly developed, pure intuition is the highest psychic ability there is, far surpassing clairvoyance. It is by meditating on this chakra that mystics attain states of transcendant peace and cosmic consciousness. In such a transcendant state there is no effort involved in practicing psychic disciplines or utilizing psychic abilities, and you can receive information, without questions or difficulties, by simply looking within.

The seventh is also the chakra used by spiritist mediums when they leave their bodies and permit spirits to speak through them. Trance mediumship is somewhat complex and can be dangerous to the unprepared. Because of the tricky nature of trance mediumship, it should not be studied through books but only under the direct guidance and supervision of an experienced trance medium or teacher.

Then there are four secondary chakras. They are located in the palms of the hands and in the arches of the feet.

The feet chakras help maintain a person's connection with the Earth, which creates the vitally important balance between the Earth energies and the cosmic energies which are pulled in through the seventh chakra. Closed feet chakras are frequently the cause of cold feet and, by restricting the amount of Earth energy allowed into the body, can cause a person to feel vague and "spaced out," or not really "all here."

Many trance mediums work with their feet entirely off the ground to minimize their connection with the material plane. Many beginning psychic students are advised to take one- or two-mile walks every day in order to focus psychic attention on the feet chakras and to open them.

The hand chakras are the seats of creative energy, located precisely at the center point between the thumb and the index finger. They are the chakras brought into play whenever we make or do something, and many psychic readers and healers use their hands both to receive and to communicate healing information and energy.

There are other specific forms which psychic reading can use, but the aura and the chakras are nearly always the primary texts.

### The Healer/Client Relationship

As you might imagine, the relationship between the reader/healer and his subject is a unique and often intimate one. If I come to you for a healing, I am giving my consent for you to learn things about me which I may have withheld from my closest friends or even from myself. I am, further, giving you permission to utilize our combined energies to effect changes in my body and possibly beyond.

When I place myself in your hands I not only assume that you know what you're doing; I also assume that you will do whatever it is you do with an inordinately high degree of integrity. I assume you will not use the information you receive in any way that will cause harm to me or to anyone else. I assume that if you don't know the answer to some of my complaints you'll tell me so and not pretend for the sake of your endangered ego that you can cure cancer if what you're really good at is fixing headaches. I assume that you will not lie to me, either by omission or by commission. And I assume that you do what you do in good faith.

In a way, if you as a healer are not willing to behave ethically, this is as good a place as any to stop reading this book and to go learn something less demanding. The techniques of healing are not difficult, but being a healer requires more than technical expertise or a sensitivity to psychic states.

## Karma and Ethics

Perhaps you've heard of *karma*. Karma is the unconscious memory or knowledge of, and attachment to, unfinished relationships, unfulfilled desires, and other incomplete cycles. Its Sanskrit form means "a deed or act." Webster's Dictionary defines karma as a Buddhist or Hindu term meaning "the totality of a person's actions in one of the successive states of existence, thought of as determining his fate in the next; hence, loosely, fate, destiny." To act on the basis of deep memories and feelings ingrained in the being's memory from other lifetimes is to act out one's karma. It is equally karmic to act on the basis of deep memories and feelings held over from childhood or any other time in your life, and unrealized in the conscious mind.

"Successive states of existence" does not necessarily mean successive lives or incarnations. It also means successive moments of now. As soon as you say "now," that moment of "now" no longer exists. It is past and gone forever. Time is an arbitrary system of measurement which human beings have invented in order to make their physical lives comprehensible. But it will help you in your work as a healer to consider that there may be no such thing as time and, instead, just an infinite series of moments of "now." This is what Heraclitus, the fifth-century B.C. Greek philosopher, meant when he observed that "you can't step in the same river twice." It is also what a close friend of ours meant when he said, "Twice? You can't step in the same river *once!*"

Time bears this relationship to karma: Whatever you have been or done up until this very instant is who you are at this very instant. The old adage that advises us to live every moment as if it were our last does not mean that we should go to hell in a handcart having "fun." It means simply that we should be prepared to answer for ourselves, to ourselves—or to our guiding spirits, or to God—all of the time. There is a sense in which unethical behavior accumulates karma and makes it harder to enter into each successive moment of "now" free and unencumbered with psychic debts.

If the totality of your actions at this moment, in this

particular state of your existence, determines your fate in the next moment, that knowledge will help you to behave ethically in this moment. When you act in a way that offends your own sense of ethics, you make your work as a healer more difficult and probably less effective, because you trouble your conscience. You make your own life more difficult. You get in your own way.

At the same time, healing provides a wonderful opportunity to be ethical in your own life while helping someone else in his. To be ethical does not mean that you always have to behave the way that the "judge" part of you tells you to. That isn't any more who you really are than that part of you that might tell you to behave unethically once in a while. You are the soul beneath the judge. You are the spirit or being who is part of all and everything. You are the entity you are when you are in the state of oneness. And beneath the daily distractions of living, you already know that.

## What Is a Psychic Healing?

This brings us to the questions: Who actually does the healing? Do you do it, as the healer? Does the person you're healing do it? What of those "healing spirits" or "healing masters" you may have heard about? If you don't do the healing, how can you be unethical in the first place? And if you can be unethical, is it not possible to do serious harm as a healer?

In the sense that a healing comes from that state of being in which all is one, no one actually does a healing. A healing is something that happens, independent of anything the subject does or anything you do. Healing takes place through a condition of forces agreeing that what is now in one state of being will be altered to be in another state of being. When the healer and healee are in a state of unity, and the healee places himself in the hands of the healer, the healer focuses the attentions of both entities on the same desired result—the healing. It sometimes comes to pass that the state of being changes, and a healing occurs.

In a sense, the consciousness of everything is brought to bear through the wills of two parts of the larger one organism working in unity, and everything in the cosmos agrees on the change. This mobilization of cosmic forces feels very much like a form of directed meditation or prayer. In fact, it is prayer, and nothing less is involved than the faith that moves mountains. Healing is a process in which the healer aligns himself totally with the totally harmonious energy of the cosmos—which you may prefer to see as God—and thereby becomes a clear channel through which that energy can flow. He then directs the energy to and through his friend, with whom he is in a state of conscious and intentional unity.

The techniques in this book are partly designed to help you, the beginning healer, enter into this state of unity with your friend and with the cosmos, and to work in harmony with them.

Given the enormous energies that come into play during a psychic healing, it is almost a foregone conclusion that these energies, when abused, can wreak great havoc in the world and cause harm to another. It may be that this is so, and certainly there are recorded instances of psychics who seemed to cause damage by misusing their skills, notably the medicine men of certain primitive tribes and some "black magic" cults. Yet, we suggest that this is not the case. When we urge a system of personal ethics upon you we do it for your own benefit, rather than for that of your friends.

First of all, your abilities as a psychic healer depend on your willingness and ability to become at one with both your client and the entire cosmos. To the degree that you cannot or do not enter into such a state of unity, your skills will be thwarted. Secondly, since we have taken as a premise for our work the position that everything that happens is part of the harmonious unfolding of the cosmos, even though we may not always be aware of it, there is a sense in which it is impossible to do any "harm" as a healer.

Finally, just as you, the healer, are ultimately responsible for your experiences, so are your friends ultimately responsible for their experiences. As a healer you can do nothing *to* someone else. You can only help him to do what he was going to do anyway. If a subject's being is unwilling to be healed, there is nothing on God's green earth you can do to heal that person. This is why all the greatest healers have clients whom they cannot cure.

When you enter into harmony with someone, your communications with him at the spirit level may indicate to you that he is unwilling to be cured at that time, or that he is unwilling to be cured by you. Perhaps in paying off his karmic debts some person is destined to have the illness he consults you about. Or perhaps because of his karmic relations with some other healer, he is destined to be healed by someone other than yourself. Being in harmony with the cosmos does not necessarily mean having things the way you want them. It means having things the way they are.

In that case, you might well ask, What difference does it make whether I become a healer or not, whether I'm ethical or not, whether I use my abilities for "good" or for "evil," or, indeed, if I even go on living?

It may be hard to understand—and it may be even harder to accept—but it makes no difference at all. As we've said, you don't become a healer to become a better or a happier person. You become a healer to become a healer—because it's there—and for no other reason. It will hamper your work and cause you considerable dissatisfaction if you begin to think you know what is good for someone else. As a healer you will never be able to impose your own ideas on someone else, although if you help him to discover his own being and his own ideas, it may seem otherwise.

At the risk of making the entire healing process totally confusing, let us state unequivocally that every person's life is his own and that whatever we discover about reality as we pass through from birth to death is exactly that which we create. The great Gestalt psychologist, Fritz Perls, observed that "I am not in this world to live up to your expectations/And you are not in this world to live up to mine. . . ." As healers we take this position one small step further: I am not here to do anything at all *to* you, and you are not here to do anything at all *to* me.

The state of being at one is the reality we have obscured beneath the drama and turmoil of our daily lives. We are always at one, even though we are only occasionally aware of it. This means that I *am* you, and you *are* me. Perhaps this sounds like mystic hocus-pocus, but once you have your own experience of being at one with another, or with all others, its truth will become apparent. In part, it is the purpose of this book to guide you toward such an experience.

The eighteenth-century English poet Samuel Taylor Coleridge advocated practicing a "willing suspension of disbelief" in order to perceive the truth behind apparent fictions. To learn to be a healer, be willing to suspend your disbelief and test out what we offer for yourself. Even if it doesn't work out for you, you've lost nothing but a few hours' reading and practice time; in exchange for that you'll have some practical, first-hand experience with the realms of the psychic. But for the most part, the exercises in this book are neither tricky nor difficult. Be willing to suspend your disbelief, if necessary, and accept what happens for you.

We'd like to conclude this introduction with two warnings and an invitation. The first warning is: Do not ever, as a healer, imagine that you are a doctor, unless you come to this book with complete medical training and you are, in fact, a physician. Healers work with great and potent cosmic forces and very frequently produce measurable results. Sometimes healers cure what physicians cannot cure, and sometimes not. Sometimes healers produce results entirely different from those they thought they set out to produce. Sometimes healers don't do a damned thing. The forces with which healers work are comprehensible at some levels of being, and incomprehensible at other levels of being. They are totally controllable at some levels of being, and totally uncontrollable at others. A healer can fail, a healer can be wrong, and sometimes a healer can be sued for practicing medicine without a license and wind up doing astral travel from behind prison walls. The physical body is a complicated mechanism, and when some part of the machine is out of order it is totally fitting and proper to send it to a qualified mechanic—which the physician is. If a person comes to you with cancer, do any psychic work with him that you can. And urge him to seek out appropriate medical advice and treatment meanwhile.

The second warning is: Healing is only one way in which you can manifest your psychic abilities. It's one direction among many which will inspire your psychic growth. However it is *only* one direction, and developing your healing abilities is developing only one facet of your larger self. If you become caught up in "being a healer," you are trapped in the veils of illusion, and you can cut yourself off from a still fuller, richer development along the road to a more total fulfillment. It will help you to remember that you aren't doing anything except what's there; it will free you to do whatever else is also there along the path of your development. It is not important to be a healer, any more than it is important to be a doctor, a plumber, or a skid-row wino. It is just a thing to be. Stay open. Use your abilities to grow rather than to stagnate in the ego-obsession that, because you're a healer, you're better than someone else, or better than you were before you became a healer.

And the invitation is: Being a psychic healer is one step along a rewarding road full of adventure, in which you can serve yourself by serving others. It is constantly exciting to discover more and more of yourself, and to discover the amazing abilities that are your birthright as a human being. To be a healer requires very little of you—only a willingness to be yourself.

# 2

## HOW TO DO SOME
## SIMPLE HEALINGS

Psychic energy is powerful stuff. It is not a toy. But then, it needn't be scary or mysterious either. As you may have gathered by now, there are countless healing styles and techniques used by everyone from Cabala scholars to the !Kung tribesmen of Botswana, Africa. Indeed, everyone who practices healing finally relies on a school that is entirely his or her own. But along the road to becoming a healer, everyone studies the art as it has been practiced by someone else already. As with any other art or science, it is easier—and more effective—to generate your own approach after you have mastered the basic skills which are already known to work.

In this chapter we are going to teach you the basic steps for performing a simple healing, for healing with visualization techniques, and for doing an "absent" healing, which is a healing on a person who is not in your physical presence. We will also discuss healing with spirit guides and psychic surgery, although we will not go into great detail about the methodology of these last two forms.

## Energy

To help yourself in working through the exercises which follow, you should get to know some terminology. To begin with, we talk a lot about "energy" in this book. By "energy" we mean roughly the same thing the Chinese mean when they speak of "chi," or the Hindus, when they speak of "prana," or Wilhelm Reich, when he speaks of "orgone." In simple day-to-day terms, you may think of "energy" as "vibrations"—good, bad, or otherwise. Energy is simply that magical, invisible stuff the cosmos is full of, for which virtually every language has a word, and which no one seems to be able to explain.

In talking about energy, we make distinctions between "Earth" energy, "cosmic" energy, "healing" energy, and so on. The sub-categories of energy are pretty much self-explanatory: Earth energy is the energy of the planet Earth, cosmic energy is the energy of the cosmos, and so on. One of our operating principles—and one which is supported by highly advanced theories of particle physics—is that everything in the universe is made up of energy, and that this energy, while it is all the same stuff, takes different forms at different times. For example, some energy takes the form of a piece of wood, and some energy takes the form of a lamb chop. Both these forms of energy can be transmuted —changed—by the process of combustion. When you burn a piece of wood its energy takes the form of heat, smoke, ash, and so on. When you eat a lamb chop its energy takes the form of you.

## Grounding

Secondly, we talk about "grounding." Grounding is a simple and surprisingly powerful technique for getting and/or staying in touch with Earth energy. It is important in all phases of meditation or psychic work as a means of keeping your being in touch with its physical manifestation, which is your body. And the psychic levels of being really can be mastered only from a thoroughly grounded place. Actually, the only time in your life you would be better off not grounded than grounded is when you're trying to levitate.

To ground yourself, sit in a straight-backed chair with your feet flat on the floor. Remove everything from your lap. Keep your arms and legs uncrossed, and place your hands on your thighs, preferably palms up. Close your eyes, relax, and clear your mind of clutter as best you can.

Now, imagine a cord or pole (string, rope, wire, wood, or whatever else appears in your mind's eye) of energy running from the base of your spine if you're a man, or from between your ovaries if you're a woman (that is to say, from your first chakra), and connecting with the deep center of the Earth. If you live on the twentieth story of some urban high-rise, just pass that cord right down through your neighbors' apartments, through all the levels of steel, stone, and glass. Psychic energy is not obstructed by such things. Repeat this exercise until you're comfortable with it. Your "grounding cord" will assure your body that it is safely connected with Mom Earth, and in its physical security it will more readily accept the new psychic energies to which you will submit it.

When Bill was learning to be a healer he had to work on this exercise for several days. Every time he put down his grounding cord it curved back up, or ran out, before it reached the center of the Earth. He was not very grounded in those days, and had to train himself to be connected with the Earth. Don't worry if it takes a little time to get used to this process. Grounding is such an invaluable tool in healing that it's worth taking the time to be sure you can do it easily and comfortably—which you will, through practice.

## Visualization

Two paragraphs ago we told you to "imagine" a cord. We explained that by referring to your "mind's eye." "Imagining" (which comes from the word "image"), "picturing," and "visualizing" are all words for the same process of creating a psychic picture. Visualization is one of the most potent and widely used techniques in healing. It has been stressed for centuries in schools of Eastern mysticism and is used in nearly every contemporary school of "consciousness-raising."

It is not necessary to see pictures clearly in order to be psychic, or to heal. In fact, while some people find picture-making easy, others never really get a clear image. But most people find that visualization becomes easier with a little practice, and the more readily you can channel your psychic energy by concentrating fully on a mental image—however you achieve it for yourself—the more readily you can translate that image into the physical reality of a healing.

Lastly, when you're working as a healer you will generally be in a very light "trance" state. At least while you're learning, it will probably help if you don't surround yourself with distractions. Don't play the radio while you heal, for instance. Take the phone off the hook. Don't chew gum or smoke. Allow yourself to be a clear channel for the psychic forces within you. And take your time. Relax and make sure you complete each step along the way, and enjoy the unfolding of a wonderful, natural gift.

### How to Do a Simple Healing

1. Have your friend sit in a straight-backed chair with his or her feet flat on the floor. This will allow the energy to flow most freely through his chakras. Have him remove everything from his lap, keep his arms and legs uncrossed, and his hands on his knees, preferably palms up. This creates an open and receptive posture. Your friend may keep his eyes open or closed, as he wishes, but he should not meditate or go into a trance state, because it will interfere with the healing. Neither of you should chew gum, smoke, or do anything else that is likely to be distracting.

2. Close your eyes for a moment, relax, clear your mind of clutter as best you can, and turn your full attention to your friend.

3. Ground yourself, and then ground your friend. You ground your friend in the same way you ground yourself: Imagine a grounding cord running from the base of his spine, or from between her ovaries, to the center of the Earth. Don't be surprised if your friend's grounding cord

44

looks different from your own: You are working with his or her energy, which may take a different form than yours takes.

4. When the first three steps have been completed, you are ready to begin the actual healing. You may open your eyes if you're more comfortable working that way, or you may work with your eyes closed.

Stand near your friend. Feel for his aura by holding your hands palms down about one foot above his head. Feel for sensations of heat, fullness, or tingling. When you see, visualize, sense, or feel the aura, start to move your hands down from the head, along the neck, shoulders, arms, torso, legs, and feet. Move your hands over the entire aura in order to compare temperatures, sensations, feelings, and images that come to your own mind.

Notice what is happening in your own body and mind as you go through this process, and learn through practice to distinguish those responses which are your own and those which reflect, in yourself, what is happening in your client. There is no technique for learning this: As you practice you will learn to rely on your sense of which is which. Learning to make this distinction is in itself a psychic process. You are learning to distinguish your intuition from your thoughts, and learning to rely on the first, while using the second as a source of information.

In moving your hands over your friend's aura, pay special attention to any part of his body in which he says or knows that he has a localized pain or ailment.

5. If parts of your friend's body feel cool, or if there is no sensation in your hands above these areas, the energy is not flowing properly there. This is frequently the case in the legs below the knees, because most people don't get sufficient exercise to support their bodies.

To correct the flow of energy, visualize orange-colored

light flowing from your hands into these cool areas. Orange, you'll recall, is one of the colors with healing properties, and it is, like the sun, warm.

The energy which flows from your hands is not "your"
energy, it is a form of neutral cosmic energy. This distinction is very important. Just as no two people look exactly
alike, so no two bodies are composed of exactly the same
form of energy. Each body can only operate properly on its
own personal brand of energy. If you give a part of yourself
—your own energy—to someone else during a healing, it
can only clog up his system while leaving you feeling
drained.

On the other hand, if you use cosmic energy to heal, it
will be clear and clean, not full of your problems, emotions,
and what you ate for breakfast. When you pass the cosmic
energy from your hands into your friend's body, it becomes
his energy. This process is something like a blood transfu-
sion, only easier. To use cosmic energy rather than your
own, you have only to will it. In Chapter 3, SELF-HEALING,
we will offer several techniques to assist you in doing this.

As we said in Chapter 1, certain colors seem to possess
specific psychic properties. Many psychics visualize colored
energy, just as we have suggested you use orange light in
this step. Color visualizations vary with the strength of the
energy you transmit. Experience will show you that there
are times you want to be delicate in your application of
color energy, and other times you want to be powerful or
even heavy-handed.

6. If parts of your friend's aura feel hot, or if the aura
seems thick or dense, there is an excess of energy in these
areas which may have accumulated in one spot because it
is blocked in some other part of the aura. There are two
ways to clear such blockages. (1) Imagine that your hands

are pulling this thick energy, like hot toffee, into the cooler areas, thereby balancing the whole aura. Or (2) imagine that you are pulling the excess heat out of the aura, where it will dissolve into neutral energy. Whichever of the two methods you use put your body into the exercise. Actually put your hands into the aura and pull the energy; actually put it where you want it. Although it may be awkward, and you may feel embarrassed at first, being active in the exercise will help to make it real for you and will strengthen the work you're doing.

7. Completing steps 5 and 6 may take you two minutes, or it may take you half an hour. Take as long as you need. When you've finished those steps, visualize a clean, clear, light golden energy flowing gently from your hands and washing over your friend's entire body. Smooth out his aura by running your hands over its edges from head to feet.

8. If your friend has had his eyes closed, have him open them now. Then have him clasp his hands together for a few minutes and just sit quietly. Clasping the hands stops the flow of energy out of the body by way of the hand chakras, and sitting quietly will allow your friend to collect himself—literally. You've just run his energy through some places it may not have been lately, and he's probably a little scattered.

While your friend is sitting quietly, visualize a magnet in front of your own aura, whose purpose is to draw back to you any of your own energy which you might have given to your friend during the healing. Remember, no one but you can use your energy, so you might as well reclaim it and not let it go to waste. Then do the same in reverse, returning to your friend any of his energy which you might have taken in during the healing. This magnet process will leave you as clean and uncluttered as when you began, and it makes the healing more effective. It's a little like sweeping up after yourself. Also, as we mentioned in step 5, it's very important to guard against trading personal energies.

This last point cannot be stressed enough. As we've told you, your friend can't use your energy and you can't use his. But there is another reason to be careful.

If you take on your friend's energy, you can also take on his illnesses—physical or mental. Doing so is an advanced form of clairsentience, or feeling how other people feel, which we discussed in Chapter 1.

For some healers, taking on another's problem is a matter of course. If such a healer works on a broken leg, he may expect to hobble around for a day or two, working out his client's ailment in his own body.

We, however, do not feel that this is *ever* necessary. The energic goop which you extract from a friend during a healing will be returned to neutral, safe, cosmic energy simply by your willing it to be so. Some healers wash their hands after a healing, to cleanse themselves of any unsavory vibrations they may have collected; others simply shake the energy off their hands periodically while they work. You should do what feels most appropriate for you. We shake our hands every so often while healing, and flick the energy away with our fingers, but other healers do not find it necessary to do so.

9. If your friend is scared after all this messing about with his psychic privates, tell a dirty joke or ask what his least favorite vegetable is. There is a 90 percent chance that it will be okra (the other 10 percent is Brussels sprouts). Since you can guess this in advance, your client will be sure you're psychic, and then he'll *really* be scared.

Many people think that this psychic jazz is magic hocus-pocus and mystic voodoo. They may very well be frightened of you and what you're doing. It will make things more pleasant for you and for your friends to end on a light note, and it will also enable them to integrate the healing into their own systems more successfully than they might otherwise. If you can avoid taking yourself too seriously (which does not mean you shouldn't take your work as a psychic seriously), you'll make it possible for your friends to overcome fear, embarrassment, allergic reactions to your cats, and their own self-importances.

10. Finally, ask your friend to bend over and let his head droop between his legs for a moment, and then stand up and have a good stretch. You do the same. Bending over allows any excess energy to flow out the seventh chakra at the top of the head and makes your body feel physical and "real" again after its psychic experience.

### Healing with Visualization

This is a basic exercise in visualization in which both you and your friend can participate actively.

1. Follow steps 1–3 from "How to Do a Simple Healing." It is helpful, but not necessary, to work all the way through step 7, so that your friend is thoroughly "cleaned out" and consequently more receptive to your further ministrations.

2. Ask your friend to make a picture in his head of how he imagines the afflicted portion of his body looks. If you are working on his overall condition or feeling, rather than on a specific part of his body, ask him to make a picture of his general condition or appearance as he imagines it. Then ask him to dissolve this image by allowing it to fade slowly

away. The process of creating and dissolving this picture will allow your friend to let go of the negative portions of his self-image.

3. Have your friend create a second mental picture of the painful area, or of his whole body, as it would look in a state of perfect health. Ask him to focus on this picture while you perform the healing.

4. Now create a picture for yourself of what your friend or his afflicted part would look like in a healthy condition. When your picture is complete, begin to work on your friend's aura as you did in "How to Do a Simple Healing." If you're working on a headache, hold your hands over his head; if you're working on stomach trouble, hold your hands over his stomach, etc. Work on the aura over the afflicted part of his body for several minutes, or until you have a sense that the process is completed. When you're done, dissolve your picture by allowing it to fade out, and then ask your friend to do the same with his picture.

5. Imagine a light, golden energy coursing through both your bodies.

6. End the healing by following steps 9 and 10 of "How to Do a Simple Healing."

### How to Do an Absent Healing

Absent healing is the process of sending healing energy to someone who is not in your physical presence. This may mean telling your uncle in Oshkosh that at 8:00 P.M. you would like to send some orange light to him to heal his trick knee. Or it may mean sending psychic energy to someone without his being aware of what you're doing.

The second example brings up an important ethical

question: Is it cricket to work on someone without his full knowledge and permission? As a general rule, our answer is "no." It isn't *wrong* to do so, since no one can receive your psychic tinkering without agreeing to it at the level of his being. But illness, like health, is a matter of individual choice. It is, in a sense, psychic good manners to keep your hands to yourself. Most people would not consider it neighborly to secretly rearrange the furniture in a friend's house because it didn't suit their own taste. It is no more considerate to rearrange someone else's energy body without his consent.

Many beginning psychics find the temptation to practice on everything and everybody irresistible: Plants, animals, sickly-looking characters on the bus—everyone becomes a subject. But this kind of work amounts to nothing but meddling. The psychic does it for his own gratification and not for the other person's benefit.

If someone is sick, that is his own business. If a person comes to you for a healing, then it becomes your business together. It's as simple as that. You cannot make someone better against his will, and some part of him will be good and angry if you try.

There are, of course, times when absent healing is appropriate. If you have communicated with the person you intend to work on, and he has verbally agreed to, or requested, a healing, you are ready to proceed. The technique suggested below is simple, and similar to "Healing with Visualization" (page 49).

1. If you wish, set a date and time with your friend and ask him to do something quiet and relaxing while you work on him. This is not always a desirable approach, because some people become anxious if they know the exact time you're working. Use your judgment.

2. Sit in a straight-backed chair, relax, and ground your-

self as you have learned to do in steps 1–3 of "How to Do a Simple Healing."

3. Clear your mind as well as you can, and create a mental picture of the person you are healing. If you don't know what he looks like, create a silhouette or an undetailed picture of him as you imagine he looks. It does not matter whether you know what the person actually looks like or not, as long as you know clearly who it is you're healing.

4. When your picture is satisfactorily clear, ground the person in your picture just as you would ground a person in the same room with you, using a simple visualization of the grounding cord appearing in the picture. Envision an orange light filling the picture and glowing within your absent friend's body and aura.

5. If you're working on a particular part of the body, concentrate the orange strongly on that part. Then, on a separate screen in your mind, imagine what that part of the body would look like if it were healthy. Now, still working in your mind's eye, superimpose the healthy picture over the afflicted part in your original picture.

6. Take as long as necessary to accomplish the preceding steps. When you're finished, let your pictures dissolve, and imagine a bright yellow sun entering and filling your friend's body; then do the same for your own body.

7. Complete the healing by bending over as in step 10 of "How to Do a Simple Healing."

When someone says "yes" to a healing, your role, if you wish to be a healer, is clear. But what do you do when a friend approaches you and says, "My mother is really feeling bad—she's in the hospital with a rare case of abracadabra, and nothing seems to work . . . Would you *pleeze* do me a favor and try to heal her? I'd ask her if she wants you to, but she doesn't believe in all this stuff."

If you simply can't say "no," there is one way around a psychic faux pas.

Ground yourself as in steps 1–3 of "How to Do a Simple Healing." Imagine that you are actually talking to the absent person's ailing body and tell it that you're going to send a positive, healing energy to it. Tell it that it may absorb as much of this energy as it wishes, and that the rest will simply bounce off its aura.

It may not be apparent at first but you are actually making contact and establishing communication with the ailing person on the psychic level. His conscious mind will probably not hear you, unless he is already active psychically, but your message is being received.

Once you've established contact, use your own method of sending healing energy. You may choose to imagine pleasant colors flowing toward your friend, or you may just think about his ailment being overcome and imagine him feeling happy and healthy. As we said earlier, we really recommend that you not walk around in unsuspecting people's auras with your astral hiking boots on. But if you find you must, keep your efforts light and gentle, and you may have some surprising results.

## Healing with Spirit Guides

As we mentioned in Chapter 1, there are both animist and spiritist traditions in virtually all psychic work. As we also mentioned, we favor the animist traditions because they place the psychic closer to what we regard as the real source of his abilities—himself. Yet, the spiritist tradition is a long and noble one, with many successful adherents.

"Spirit guides," or "healing guides," or "healing masters," are the helpmates and advisors of a great many healers. In the popular lexicon, "spirits" are also known as "ghosts." We prefer the former term, because "ghost" conjures up all sorts of spooky and fallacious Halloween imagery.

Both the spiritist and the animist traditions work with the premise that all persons have a "soul" or a "being" which is, in a sense, immortal and which "inhabits" the body during a lifetime. When a person dies and the physical form has completed its cycle on Earth, the being lives on, on some other plane of existence which we loosely call the "astral" plane. The being goes on to take other physical forms and to live other lives, entering a new body at birth each time it reincarnates.

Each person has a subconscious (and, for some, a conscious) recollection of his past lives. In some traditions, where past, present, and future are all seen as different facets of the same, timeless "now," people are thought to have subconscious "recollections" of their future lives as well. This version of the reincarnational theory explains *prescience*, which is the ability to know the future.

Between incarnations—between the death of one body and the birth of the next one which a particular being will inhabit—the being is out of a body altogether. In its astral state the being retains all the information and experience it gleaned from its many incarnations, without all the strong emotions that go along with being physical. Many spirits who worked on Earth as healers of one sort or another maintain an interest in their studies and continue to learn on the astral plane.

Out of a wish to practice its skills, or karmic indebtedness, or simply friendship and goodwill, a spirit may choose to work with people in bodies. This arrangement can be advantageous to both parties: The healer receives the benefit of the spirit's knowledge and expertise; the spirit, who is not as strong and effective on the physical plane when operating without a body as someone is while in a body, can have a greater effect by working through another's existing body.

How does a healer acquire a spirit assistant? Some healers tell of being approached by spirits, or seeing visions. Others make the initial contacts themselves by tuning into the spirit world and requesting assistance. Still others claim the spirits are just there.

In any case, the first step in healing with spirit guides is for the healer to get in contact with the being or beings with whom he will work. (Sometimes the spirit will identify itself by sex or by name, to make the process of meeting with the healer easier.) The healer then holds his hands over the subject's body and asks his spirit guide to focus on his hands and work through them.

The healer may open himself to the suggestions of the spirit and allow his hands to be guided. Such guidance may range from the healer's having a mild sense of knowing which directions to move in, to a strong sense of magnetism which literally seems to pull the healer's hands to and fro about the client's aura, or to rest them suspended over a particular spot. Other healers prefer to choose the placement of their own hands and then give directions to their guides. When the healer feels that his work is finished, or receives an indication from the spirit that the work is complete, he asks the spirit to depart.

A discorporate entity will usually communicate with a healer in one of two ways. The first, which we have just described, is most easily seen as a kind of "intuition" on the healer's part. The second is called *clairaudience,* or "clear

55

hearing," which is hearing voices of out-of-body beings, or even carrying on conversations with them.

Clairaudience is not quite like hearing with your ears; it is more a matter of hearing with your "inner" ear—as when you think to yourself but you can perceive that you're not just chatting with yourself. Many people who hear voices and think they're crazy are actually just clairaudient without knowing it.

The phenomenon of psychic hearing is not easily described, and not all practicing psychics possess, or utilize, this ability. Sometimes the skill can be developed by practice, but for many people it is simply too peculiar or too frightening, and other avenues of psychic exploration yield more concrete results. To those who are clairaudient and use their ability, healing guides can give psychic, psychological, and nutritional advice for their clients, as well as instructions about where to place their hands.

None of these spiritist practices is to be confused with trance mediumship, which takes place when the spirit enters directly into the body of the clairvoyant or healer. While many mediums do have spirits working through them, the process of the work is completely different from the process of using spirit guides. Mediumship, as we said in Chapter 1, can be dangerous and should not be regarded as a mere party game.

Nor, for that matter, should you attempt to heal with a spirit guide unless you are under the personal supervision of an experienced spiritist healer. While there may be much to learn through sharing with friends both in and out of bodies, the object of all psychic work is to become—or, more accurately, to recognize that you already are—the total creator yourself, developing your own power and freedom of choice.

Discorporate entities are learning, just as you are. They do not always have the solution to a problem that has you stumped. Being out of a body is not superior to being in a body; it is simply another way of being. Not all ghosts are holy, and many amateur spiritists have made the mistake of giving up their own personal sense of responsibility because they thought that a spirit would somehow know better than they. Out-of-body beings can lose their sense of what it is like to operate on the physical plane. Getting run over by a bus won't hurt *them*, but it might bring your own ministry to an untimely end.

Being "possessed" by a spirit, or having your house haunted, is basically the result of your own inability to say "no." Learning to say "no" is a very useful skill to develop in psychic work. While you would probably ask someone to leave your house if you wanted them gone, it doesn't occur to many people that they can say the same thing to an out-of-body tenant.

A couple of years ago a friend of Bill's was killed by an automobile in Chicago. The night she died, Bill found her everywhere in his own home. When he walked into the bathroom, she was lying in the tub. When he went to the living room, she was sitting in his favorite chair. When he went to his desk, she tried to speak to him. Finally, he sat down and told her that, while he loved her deeply and regretted that they would not be able to play on the physical plane any more, he could not have her hanging around his apartment; she would have to realize that she was dead, and had other fish to fry. She vanished immediately and has only returned a few times, for a few minutes each time, to say hello.

All most ghosts really want is a little communication. As one of our teachers so aptly put it, "Why be scared of a being so lonely and frightened that it has to live in a closet?"


## Psychic Surgery

Neither of us are psychic surgeons, and you will find no instruction on how to perform psychic surgery in this book. But the growing popularity and notoriety of the subject demand that we say a little something about it here. It is, after all, a method of psychic healing.

Psychic surgery means exactly what its name implies—actual surgery without surgical instruments, tools, hospitals, or anesthetic drugs. The surgeon places his bare hands on his patient's body, inserts his fingers into the ailing flesh, and makes the necessary adjustments, frequently withdrawing lumps of diseased tissue or foreign bodies. When he is finished (the entire operation may take only a couple of minutes, and rarely goes as long as half an hour), the wound closes completely with a mere pass of the surgeon's hand over it, and there is little or no scar. The operation is ordinarily entirely painless.

Incredible as it may seem, many thousands of people have been helped by this method of healing. The widespread use of psychic surgery in the Philippine Islands has popularized it elsewhere, where there are few psychic surgeons.

Perhaps the most famous psychic surgeon is Tony Agpaoa, who practices in the Philippines. His remarkable reputation for success inspires many desperate Europeans and

Americans to make the costly trip to the Islands to see him. His operations are bloody, but while normal blood-clotting takes eight to ten minutes, when Tony works, the blood clots in seconds.

Many psychic surgeons claim that it is not necessary to open the body at all (and many do not draw blood), but that they do it to make the operation more believable. As one of Tony's students, Rosita Rodriguez, says, "You have to understand that when a person spends fifteen hundred to two thousand dollars to make a trip eleven thousand miles away to see a little bit of blood in order to believe that they were healed, Tony *has* to open the body. It was originally meant for the primitive peoples, but the Americans stumbled onto it and decided that this was *it.* They all want the show of blood."

When the surgeon's fingers have entered the body, they "magnetically" draw the diseased tissue to them. For some surgeons, it is not even necessary to enter the body near the afflicted areas—the magnetism will draw the impurity from any part of the body.

No one really seems to know what makes the surgeon's fingers enter the unresistant flesh. It may be that energy shifts its form from one kind of matter to another. The late Reverend Harold Plume, a psychic surgeon in Monterey, California, said, "Hoo Fang [Reverend Plume's spirit healing guide] told me that he disintegrates my fingers by vibrating them very rapidly. You know if you took this sofa and vibrated it fast enough it would disintegrate. So it's the same with my fingers. And when my fingers, in that fast state, touch another person's body they also feel that vibration, and that part of *their* body disintegrates. That's why the energy is allowed to slip right in without a scar and without blood. It's the darndest thing. . . ."

Or perhaps, as the Indian yogis claim when they painlessly place nails and knives into their bodies, they are simply passing between the cells.

# 3

# SELF-HEALING

When you have a headache and it goes away, you are the person who healed you. When you cut your finger and it heals, you are the person who healed you. When you catch a cold at night and then feel better the next morning, you are the person who healed you.

Self-healing is an entirely normal and natural process. It is so much a part of having a body that, for most small ailments and some larger ones as well, we consign the healing work to the autonomic nervous system—that unconscious part of ourselves that also controls our breathing, our digestion, the beating of our hearts, and the replacement of all the cells in our bodies every seven years.

The principal difference between autonomic healing and self-healing as we'll discuss it here is that, in the techniques that follow, abilities that now lie dormant or unnoticed within you will begin to become conscious, and, as a result, you'll begin to have control over them.

## Awakening

In virtually all psychic, consciousness, and mystical traditions, the first step to realizing your own individual power is the process of "awakening." It is the theory behind these schools of thought that, for the most part, we all walk around in a more or less unconscious state of mind. The great Armenian mystic, G. I. Gurdjieff, called this state "being asleep," and indeed, when you begin to "awaken" it truly does feel as if you'd been merely dreaming your life away. The Bible describes the process of awakening as "scales" falling from the eyes, because when you awaken you suddenly begin to see and understand things in ways that have previously been hidden from you, or incomprehensible to you.

The first step in awakening—which, for our purposes, is the first step in actualizing your healing abilities—is the process of observation. This simply means that you notice what goes on with you at all times. It does not mean that you make judgments about yourself or others, and it does not mean you change, or try to change, the ways in which you behave or someone else behaves. It only means that you notice your responses to yourself, to others, and to the world at large. Notice what makes you happy, what makes you sad, what makes you angry, bored, excited, and most of all, notice what puts you to "sleep"—what happens in your life to prevent you from being in present time—being "here now."

As they begin to observe themselves, most people find that they tune in for a few seconds and then tune out for several hours; then they remember that they're observing themselves and they tune in again for a few seconds and tune out again for several hours. Eventually—sometimes after a few days, usually after a few weeks, occasionally right away—if they continue to do this exercise they begin to tune in for longer periods of time and tune out for shorter ones. They also begin to tune in more frequently and tune out less frequently. P. D. Ouspensky, one of Gurdjieff's most prominent students, called this the process of "remembering" himself.

The process of self-observation activates the sleeping portions of the mind which we know as the "subconscious." When this part of the mind wakes up, it releases an enormous store of untapped power in an individual. This is the power of the psychic realm, and its release often signals a person's increased satisfaction with his life, and an increased ability to control the rate and direction of his own psychic growth. It is the beginning of self-knowledge, which all history's wise men have shown to be the first step toward personal liberation from the prisons we make of our own lives.

The process of self-healing begins with self-observation. In this chapter we will discuss a variety of techniques for use in self-healing. These techniques all involve some form of self-observation, and as healing techniques they are applicable for treating everything from a stubbed toe to cancer.

You can proceed with these exercises, and with all the rest of the exercises in this book, as you observe yourself. Self-observation knows neither temporal nor spatial limits. You can observe yourself any time, anywhere. It is an ongoing process which will open doors for you as long as you do it, and you don't have to reach any particular level of self-awareness to continue with other exercises or other forms of learning. When you are observing yourself, everything in your life becomes part of your growth process.

## Pain and Disease

Pain and disease result from disruptions or imbalances in your life energy. Such disruption or imbalance may come from a single upset, from a series of small irritations, or from some old, forgotten conflict that was never fully resolved in your life. It can also result from a more immediate experience. For instance, if you've just spent some time with someone you regard as a tiresome bore, don't be surprised if you get a pain in the neck. An unrequited love may indeed leave you heartsore.

The part of your body that becomes afflicted is communicating a message to you. For example, a disease of the sex organs bespeaks a reluctance to have sex; a sore throat or laryngitis points to a wish not to communicate; eye disease to a desire not to see what is going on around you or in your own life; shoulder and back pains suggest that you are carrying life's burdens on your shoulders or back.

Because disease shows up in the psychic, or astral, body before it shows up in the physical body, a psychic reader can often diagnose an illness before it occurs, or at least can know that an illness is coming on. This ability applies equally to work with yourself or work with others.

Illness is a process by which your body communicates information to you about imbalances and disruptions you are making, or allowing to be made, in your life. When you read that an illness is approaching, you can ask yourself what is out of order in your psychic space, and what you can do to correct the imbalance.

The process of being ill is, of course, part of the process of being well, and sometimes you may have to go ahead and have your disease. Still, "an ounce of prevention is worth a pound of cure." If you are able to get some psychic information about yourself, you can often avoid an illness, or alleviate it, by asking your body what it needs to regain its psychic balance and then giving it that.

For many years, Bill suffered with a weak back. Once or twice a year he would wake up almost unable to move and would have to spend a couple of days in bed staring at the ceiling. Medical men were befuddled. X-rays showed nothing wrong with his spine, and back specialists couldn't find anything wrong with the musculature in his back. A chiropractor stretched his spine, and while Bill enjoyed growing an inch in two minutes, he was still in abysmal pain half an hour later.

Finally, two things cleared up his back trouble—permanently, it seems. One of these things was being Rolfed—a method of deep-muscle manipulation which is more obviously physical than it is psychic. The other thing was that he began to have psychic conversations with his back. He said, *Okay, back, what's going on? What do you want from me that you're not getting?* And his back replied, *Love me.* I love you, Bill said. *You're my one and only back.*

His back whimpered, *You don't love me the right way. You walk funny, which puts strain on me, and you sit funny, which puts more strain on me. More to the point, you never give me any rest. You're always doing doing doing. You never stop and sit and simply be. Every part of your body and mind needs a chance to just stop*

65

*and unwind from time to time, and I'm your body's spokesman. I
don't mean take a lot of vacations, I mean just lay off for a few
minutes every hour or so. Recharge yourself.*

And so Bill began to pay attention to his back. He noticed
that after a long day it would twitch, and he recognized that
it—and he—was tired. So he would simply lie down on the
floor, on his back, for a few minutes and feel the twitching
go away. That's about the time his body told him to go get
Rolfed. And Bill and his back have lived happily ever after.

This tale of love and passion doesn't sound particularly
psychic. Indeed, the whole experience was very physical for
Bill. But the direction the cure took came from information
Bill got from himself psychically. And he got the information simply by asking and by trusting himself to tell himself
the truth. When we talk about "owning" your health and
your illnesses, and say that you have created them both in
your life, this is the sort of thing we mean. Trust yourself.
You know more than you think you know.

Let's get down to some brass tacks. Everything you've
learned so far about healing others is directly applicable to
healing yourself as well—just as the techniques that follow
in this chapter are applicable to healing other people. Healing your friend *is* healing yourself, and healing yourself *is*
healing your friend. The first technique is very similar to
"How to Do a Simple Healing," in Chapter 2.

## How to Do a Simple Self-Healing

1. Sit in a straight-backed chair with your feet flat on the
floor. Take everything off your lap, keep your arms and legs

uncrossed, and place your hands on your thighs, preferably palms up. Don't chew gum, smoke, play the radio, etc. (Hereafter, we'll call this step "sitting in the psychic posture," or "going into trance.")

2. Close your eyes, relax, clear your mind as best you can, and turn your full attention to yourself.

3. Ground yourself.

4. Starting from your head, imagine your aura. (It doesn't matter whether you can see it or not. We'll go into reading auras in the next chapter.) In your imagination, follow your aura down from your head, along your neck, shoulders, arms, torso, legs, and feet. You are simply working to get a "feel" or a "sense" of your aura in your mind. If you see, visualize, sense, or feel a thin or cool part of your aura, or cool colors, or cool images (icebergs are cool; so is a picture of yourself being very worldly and sophisticated: the mind is a merciless punster), or if you receive no impressions at all when you reach some particular part of your aura, the energy is not flowing properly there. Visualize neutral, orange-colored light flowing into these areas.

If parts of your aura seem hot to you, or thick, or dense, too much energy has accumulated in these parts because of blocks in other parts of your aura. Clean out this excess energy in exactly the same way you did for your friend in "How to Do a Simple Healing" except you need not dig into your own aura with your hands. In this case, simply imagine that you're doing so. But imagine thoroughly.

5. When you've completed step 4, and the energy is flowing well throughout your aura, visualize a clear, clean, neutral, light golden energy washing over your entire body.

6. Starting from your head and working down to your feet, imagine your own hands smoothing out your aura.

7. Open your eyes, clasp your hands, and sit quietly for

a moment. Then bend over and let your head hang between your legs for a minute or so. Finally, stand up and
have a good stretch. If you feel a little vague or "spaced
out," walk around for a couple of minutes before going out
into the world again. (Hereafter, we'll call this step "coming out of trance.")

## Running Energy

In Chapter 1 we talked very briefly about energy and
about utilizing a proper balance of Earth and cosmic energies to maintain psychic stability. The process we were
referring to is known as "running energy." Running energy
is an ideal way to recharge your batteries, to restore your
energy balance if it becomes disrupted by the rigors of daily
life, or to give your energy system a general cleaning out.
Although we have no particular recommendation about
running energy on a regular basis—do so if you wish, and
don't if you don't—we will acknowledge that it's a great way
to set yourself up at the start of the day, or to mellow out
after eight hours in the mines. Finally, it will serve you well
to run energy before and after doing long healings, first to
establish, and later to reestablish, your psychic equilibrium.

a. *How to Run Earth Energy*
  1. Follow steps 1–3 from "How to Do a Simple Self-
Healing."
  2. When you're well grounded, focus your attention on
your feet chakras (located, you'll recall, in the arches of
your feet). Imagine the light brown energy of the planet
Earth being drawn up through your feet chakras, and

spreading up your lower legs, your thighs, and into your first chakra (at the base of the spine in men, between the ovaries in women). You may literally *feel* this energy—many people do.

3. Now imagine the Earth energy traveling up into your body, passing through your second, third, fourth, fifth, sixth, and seventh chakras. Send some of it out to your hand chakras. Imagine it flowing into your aura.

4. When the energy reaches your seventh chakra, at the top of your head, bring it back down through your body. When, on its return trip, it reaches your first chakra, flush it straight down your grounding cord into the center of the Earth, where it will be neutralized, carrying all sorts of your psychic garbage with it.

5. Come out of your trance.

b. *How to Run Earth and Cosmic Energy*
When you can run Earth energy comfortably, and you know the steps well enough so you don't have to refer to this book to do it, add some cosmic energy to the mixture.

1. Follow steps 1–3 of "How to Run Earth Energy."

2. While the Earth energy is traveling through your body, focus on your seventh (crown) chakra, at the top of your head. Imagine the golden energy of the cosmos being pulled down through your crown, entering your seventh chakra, and traveling directly down to your third chakra, at your solar plexus.

3. Now imagine the Earth energy and the cosmic energy meeting in your third chakra, and mix them together like a malted milk.

4. When you have the two energies mixed together, send the mixture flowing throughout your body. Keep the mixture circulating for a minute or two, then ground it out—

that is, send it down your grounding cord to the center of the Earth.

5. Come out of your trance. Hereafter, when we talk about "running energy," we mean running Earth and cosmic energy together, as you've just done.

### Opening and Closing the Chakras

Usually, when we tell people we're going to teach them to open and close their chakras, their minds go all rubbery trying to figure out what we're talking about and being certain that they'll never be able to do it—whatever it is. Relax. You just did it.

In the previous exercise, when you brought Earth energy up through your feet chakras, you opened them. After all, the energy couldn't be expected to enter through a closed psychic door, could it? Similarly, when you brought cosmic energy down through your crown, you opened your seventh chakra. Opening and closing the chakras is entirely a matter of will: You simply do it. You can use a mental picture to help with this.

Ordinarily, you run your chakras automatically by a kind of astral device that regulates the flow of energies into and out of your psychic system, just as your autonomic nervous system keeps air coming in and out of your lungs and blood running around your veins and arteries. Sometimes, however, it's to your advantage to be able to control the energy entering your system, or to open or close a particular chakra.

Back in Chapter 1, for instance, when we began talking about chakras, we talked about one kind of trouble you can run into by having a wide-open second. If that same friend who has lots of problems wants to have coffee with you, and you want to help him without taking on his depression, all you have to do is close down your second chakra by at least half, and you'll be much less likely to go "into sympathy" with him. Then you're free to listen to his troubles and, if you both wish, to offer support and advice. And when you part, you'll still feel fine: You won't be carrying his psychic baggage with you.

You want your energies to serve you, not to be in conflict with you. You want your energy centers to operate in a manner that's appropriate to a given situation. For instance, if you've been "in survival" for a long time, handling your rent, your job, getting enough to eat, and so on, and then one day you have plenty of money and the landlord sends you a bouquet of roses, it's no longer appropriate to be in survival. You're surviving just fine. But your first chakra may not know this right away. It's been operating at top capacity for a few weeks or a few months, and it's used to being 100 percent open.

If you let the situation ride, your first will eventually close down by itself. But in the meantime you may be running around anxious and tense because you're still operating out of survival. It's much easier simply to close down the chakra when you know it's time to do so and reopen it when you need it. The same holds true for every chakra.

Here's a little exercise to give you the feel of opening and closing the chakras. It's a little bit like trying out the flaps on an airplane. When you get used to your ability to control these energy centers, you can open or close them any time.

1. Sit in the psychic posture, clear your mind, and ground yourself.

2. Focus your attention on your first chakra. As we said

in Chapter 1, the chakras generally appear as small, dully colored disks about the size of a silver dollar. If yours look different, there's nothing to worry about. We've seen chakras that looked like pinwheels, old coins, bottle tops, pyramids, and all kinds of other shapes. If you can't see your chakra, just pretend you can, and imagine what it would look like if you *could* see it.

3. Imagine your first chakra opening up like an iris in a camera lens, or like a flower opening its petals.

4. When your first is open as far as it will go comfortably, imagine it slowly closing until it's completely shut.

5. Now imagine the chakra opening again.

6. Imagine the chakra closing again.

7. Repeat steps 3–6 until you have a clear sense of what your first feels like when it's open, and what it feels like when it's closed.

8. Repeat the entire exercise with each of your seven major chakras, and then with the hand chakras, and finally with the feet chakras. Take as much or as little time as you need to complete each step. Eventually, you'll find that you can open or close any chakra instantly, simply by willing it.

9. When you've completed this entire exercise, take one last look at each of your chakras and determine how much you want it to be open—completely, 1/2, 1/4, 10 percent, or whatever—and tell it to be open that much. Don't close any of your chakras down completely for now.

10. Come out of your trance.

## Being in the Corner of the Room

This is an exercise designed to let you know that you are totally in control of your energy focus. In addition to honing your general psychic abilities, this exercise will be useful when you do readings (see Chapter 4), when you do out-of-body healings (see Chapter 8), and in self-diagnosis.

1. Sit in the psychic posture, clear your mind, and ground yourself.

2. Staying grounded, open your eyes for a moment and look at the four corners of the room where the walls meet the ceiling.

3. Pick any one of the corners and close your eyes again.

4. Imagine that you are in that corner, looking down at your body sitting in its chair. Stay there for a minute or so. Imagine what your body looks like from the corner of the room. What is it doing? Imagine that you can see your aura surrounding your body. What does it look like? If you can't see it, what would it look like if you *could* see it?

5. Imagine that you are back in your body, in the center of your head. How does it feel there? Does it feel any different than being in the corner of the room felt? If so, how?

6. Go back and forth between your body and the corner of the room several times. Each time you're in the corner, take a look at your body and imagine your aura surrounding it—or imagine you're imagining it.

7. Come out of your trance.

Don't work on this exercise for more than 15 minutes at a time, but do it often enough that you feel comfortable being in your body and being in the corner of the room. Don't practice this exercise while driving.

## Color Meditation and Color Healing

In the previous chapters of this book we have instructed you to use colored healing energies. So far you've used light brown Earth energy, golden cosmic energy, and orange healing energy.

It is widely known that color can affect mood: The packaging and brightly colored displays in the supermarket are geared toward making the consumer want to buy; the dark brown woods of a country cabin give a cozy, earthy feeling; a room decorated in sedate blues and greens is soothing, while a room papered and furnished in garish reds and oranges creates the opposite effect. When you plan, at night, to wear a black and white dress the next day, and in the morning you change your mind and opt for pink, you are matching your clothing to your change of mood.

To find out how different colors affect you, try the following color meditation.

First, ground yourself. Then, instead of going into trance by bringing in Earth and cosmic energies, run *colored* energy. Using the colors in the following list, first visualize a blob of one color on your mental screen, and then imagine that color going up through your feet and legs and down through your crown, and circulate it throughout your body. Spend 30 seconds to a minute on each color, then let it fade out and bring in the next one. We recommend this order:

1. Black is the color you'll begin with, then switch to
2. Gray. Notice the difference. Now bring in
3. Brown. Start with a light brown, then imagine it deepening. Next is
4. Red. Again, start with a light red and watch it become a rich scarlet. Follow that with

74

5. Orange, with which you are already familiar. Does orange feel different to you while you're doing this exercise than it has in previous exercises? Next, bring in

6. Yellow. Follow yellow with a

7. Light Apple Green. Darken it into a rich sea green. The next color is

8. Sky Blue. Deepen it slowly until it is a royal blue. Follow this with

9. Pink. From pink go to

10. Lavender. Deepen this into

11. Purple. After purple run

12. Gold. After gold,

13. Silver. And after silver,

14. White.

Come out of trance.

As you do this meditation, notice which colors feel most comfortable to you. When you sit down to run energy, or to do any of the self-healing exercises in this chapter, you might take a moment at the beginning to run a color you like through your body. It is not necessary to repeat the entire exercise to reach your color—just imagine it appearing spontaneously, and proceed as you normally do when running energy.

Using colors to heal others is highly effective. Simply imagine the color of your choice (you've already done this with orange, remember) flowing through your hands (once again, do *not* use your own energy) into your friend's body and/or chakras and aura. To determine the color of your choice, and to determine when to use a color other than orange—the basic color—intuition and practice will be your best guides. We find that orange is not too strong and gives pep, while blue is soothing for someone who is nervous.

If your friend is well grounded, you cannot affect him adversely with too much energy. Any more than he can use will go down his grounding cord. However, it really will make things easier if you are sensitive to starting off with the right amount of energy. Even though your friend may claim he doesn't feel a thing you do, you are *not* playing with a toy: The energy you direct is affecting his astral body and his physical one. You would not give a pizza to a person who hadn't eaten in a week—you'd be wise to start with something light, like juice, and work your way up to a pizza. Don't give your friends astral indigestion. Start out softly and work up to the stronger colors and the more powerful techniques.

### Making the Body Real

By now you may have noticed that we conclude each exercise with the same step—we ask you to clasp your hands and sit quietly for a moment, and then to bend over and let your head dangle between your legs for a minute or so. Sometimes we also suggest that you walk around the room after doing these other steps.

As we said earlier, the purpose of clasping your hands after doing psychic work is to make the body into a closed psychic circuit so that energy doesn't flow out of you randomly. Bending over allows excess psychic energy—that which *should* leave your body—to spill out. Walking around is one way of making your body "real" again after you engage in psychic activities.

76

We don't mean to suggest that your body becomes less "real" while you're working than at other times. Rather, when you do psychic work you focus your attention on your astral, rather than on your physical, body. It makes it easier to operate on the physical plane after doing such work if you first reaffirm your connection with your physical body.

Running psychic energy through a body inevitably shakes up the works. At some point in following the procedures in this book, you will probably have new insights and new attitudes toward yourself and others. As you get to know your body in this way, you may find that some of its feelings and reactions are based on other people's considerations of what is best for you, instead of your own, and you may wish to live more fully from your own will.

All this represents change to a body, and a body's first reaction to change is to say "No!" This is because, whatever a body's habits are—good or bad, better or worse— these are what it *knows*. And if it thinks that what it knows is going to be taken away from it, it goes into survival. In an extreme case, a body may get sick. More often it may feel drowsy, or restless, or bored, or scared as you do psychic work. This is your body's way of saying "I don't want to change!"

Perhaps you're someone who gets scared or angry when shown a lot of love. When you come to realize this, you may decide, instead, to respond warmly to love. Yet, every time someone loves you, you continue to feel angry or scared. This is because your body has made a *habit* of its responses. It thinks, "This is what I've always done! This is my survival! I can't give this up!" It has to learn new patterns slowly.

As we've discussed, observing yourself is the first step in psychic growth. If you see things about yourself that you wish to change, it is certainly possible for you to do so. However, change them gently, or your body may feel unreal or unloved. Don't blame yourself for any way you have been, or are, or will be. Instead, affirm that any decisions to change are gifts to yourself from yourself, and that however you are or have been was the way that worked for you when you were that way. If something else will work better now, that is the reason to grow into it—not because you are or have been "bad."

There are many ways to make the body real, and the distinguishing feature of all of them is that they focus your attention on your body. Since it is that focus of attention you want from such an exercise, you shouldn't do it haphazardly. Instead, pay attention to what you're doing, and if you space out while doing it, see if you can recall the exact moment when that happened and what you were thinking about at that time.

These exercises are simple and fun. Beware! They are also traps. Because they're simple, and because they're fun, it's very easy to do them automatically, without paying attention.

Each of these exercises has only one step; the following list, then, is a series of different exercises, not a single exercise with several steps.

1. Eat something.
2. Have sex in the form of your choice.
3. Exercise. Walking is particularly good for making the body real, since it directs attention to the feet chakras, which are your immediate connection with the Earth.
4. Bathe or shower. A dousing of cold water works wonders to reacquaint the being with its body and vice-versa.

Your own body may have some particular way in which it likes to be reminded of its reality. If so, do that.

## Cords

Occasionally in this book we talk about your "space," and other people's space, and being in your own space. Your space is your body, physical and astral, and only you can occupy it comfortably. Unfortunately, other people will frequently try to horn in on it because they want you to pay attention to them or want you to give them communication of some kind.

In psychic lingo, we call other people's requests for attention "cords." The clairvoyant eye can perceive lines of energy, resembling cords, entering into the chakras and connecting you with another person. Again, it is not necessary to actually see the cords: You can simply *know* that they're there just as effectively.

Cords are passed back and forth between people's chakras constantly, without the people being aware of it. In the next exercise we will show you how to locate and remove your cords, which are usually unnecessary clutter you carry around. If you're chock full of cords, you're likely to be operating partially on other people's energy rather than on your own. It is a mistake, however, to regard "being corded" by someone as an imposition, or as something bad that is being done to you. In fact, you cannot receive another person's cords unless you're willing to do so. No one can do anything *to* you psychically: It always takes two to tango.

Cords have different meanings and different effects in the different chakras:

*First Chakra*     This is the survival center. A cord into this center means "I want you to help me survive." The first can be an unsavory place to find a cord, unless two people have a clear agreement along survival lines. For example, a child would naturally place such a cord into its parents, or into other adults central to its life. Or, if you have a friend who is sick or hurt, and you are taking care of him, you may have a clear understanding between you that for a certain amount of time you *wish* to help him survive. However, if you find a friend's or lover's cord planted in your first carrying a covert "I need you" message, you may wish to remove the cord and reexamine the nature of your relationship. Remember, no one can put a cord in you unless you are willing to receive it

*Second Chakra*     This is the chakra of sexuality and emotion. A cord in the second means either "I am interested in you sexually" or "Give me your emotional support, pay attention to my emotions." You may or may not wish to remove a sex cord, according to whether or not you're enjoying it. An emotion cord is better off removed from your chakra because it is a potential energy drain for you and is often accompanied by a "needy" vibration. It is easier to respond to someone's emotional needs from your heart chakra than from your second.

*Third Chakra*     This is the energy center. A cord here means "I want some of your energy, my own is not enough," or "I'd rather operate on your energy than be responsible for running on my own." Obviously, a cord in the third can only sap you of your own energy, and it would serve you to remove it. A strong cord in this center can cause a tight sensation in your stomach.

*Fourth Chakra*     This is the center of love and affinity.

80

A cord in the fourth usually means "I love you," or "I like you." You may wish to remove cords in the fourth, if only for the sake of being the only person with energy in your body; but in general, these cords are not as draining as others. Sometimes Amy consciously leaves fourth chakra cords in when she cleans out her chakras, because she enjoys her friends' "hello's."

*Fifth Chakra* This is the communications center. A cord here means "I want to communicate with you," and often, "I want to talk to you." A large cord in the fifth can cause you to have an ache in your throat.

*Sixth Chakra* This is the clairvoyant center. A cord in the sixth means that someone is "in your head"—that he is thinking of you intensely, or that he wonders what you're thinking about, or perhaps what you think of him. These cords can be the cause of a headache.

*Seventh Chakra* This is the chakra of knowingness and intuition. It is another unsavory location for a cord because its message is "I want to control you," or perhaps, "I want you to follow my teachings." A number of teachers in the psychic, mystic, and consciousness fields set temporary cords in the seventh chakras of their students or disciples to facilitate learning.

*Hand Chakras* The hands are the seats of creative energy, and a cord here may mean either "Do it my way," or "Do it for me." Since creativity is a form of self-expression, a cord in the hand can affect the ways in which you actualize virtually anything you do, from cooking to playing tennis to writing a book.

*Feet Chakras* The feet are your connection with the Earth, and a cord in your feet dislocates your grounding and may make you feel vague and spaced out or even "swept off your feet."

The primary advantage to knowing about cords and

knowing how to remove them is that you are a cleaner, freer agent when running your body on your own steam. A secondary advantage is that as you become more practiced in finding and removing your cords, you will learn a lot about your relationships. You may discover cords from very unexpected people in very unexpected places. Furthermore, the person who has corded you may be more or less unaware of the nature of what he or she is communicating.

How do you know if someone's corded you? Take a look at your aura and your chakras. If there are cords—and there probably are, to a greater or lesser extent—you'll see them. What do you do if you find cords in your chakras? Pull them out.

## How to Pull Cords

1. Sit in the psychic posture, close your eyes, clear your mind, and ground yourself.

2. Run energy for a minute or so.

3. Imagine your aura as you did in Step 4 of "How to Do a Simple Self-Healing," and follow the rest of the instructions for that step.

4. When you've cleaned out your aura and the energy is flowing well, focus your attention on your first chakra as you did in Step 2 of "Opening and Closing the Chakras." See if you can see, visualize, sense, or feel any cords there. If not, look again.

If you find cords in your first, imagine your hands going into your aura, into the chakra, and pulling them out. A cord can be big, small, thick, wispy, easy or difficult to remove. Be gentle! Most cords will slide right out if you want them to, and there's no point in tearing a hole in your chakra. If some cords seem stubborn, ask the cord who owns it, or follow it out from your aura until you see, visualize, sense, or feel the person who threw it to you.

This person may be a close friend or spouse; it may be your boss or employee; it may be the panhandler you gave a quarter to this morning. In fact, it could be anyone, including someone who's been dead for years. Just take a look, and assume that whoever it is who shows up in your imagination is the right person. If more than one person shows up, you're probably working on two cords at once. Put either one on "hold" until you've handled the other.

When you've traced the cord back to its owner, thank him for his interest in you and explain that you do not want to be corded; if he wants to relate to you, tell him to do so on a conscious, physical plane instead of on the astral. Then go back to your first chakra and pull the cord. It should come out without any problem. If it will not come out, no matter what you do, perhaps you don't really want to remove it. It is all right to leave the cord in, but be aware that you have made this choice. If you remove one that you really want, it will come back. Your cord-communication system already exists. The purpose of this exercise is to give you a choice about whether or not you want other people running around in your energy or imposing theirs on you.

5. When you feel free of cords in the first, move on to the second chakra. Run through step 4 with your second, and then move on through all the rest of your chakras, including the hands and feet.

6. When you've pulled the cords from all your chakras, visualize an enormous faucet of crystal-clear water washing out your energy system, pouring into your seventh chakra,

and flowing down through your sixth, fifth, fourth, third, second, and first (you can circulate it through your hands and feet as well), and then flush the water down your grounding cord to the center of the Earth, where it will neutralize.

7. Now visualize a clear, clean, neutral, light golden energy washing through your energy system and over your entire body.

8. Starting from your head and working down to your feet, imagine your own hands smoothing out your aura.

9. Come out of your trance. Do something to make your body real—wash your face, or have a cup of coffee or tea, or find a friend to hug. This is the most rigorous psychic exercise you've learned from us so far. Be nice to yourself for the rest of the day.

### Neutrality and Nonresistance

With all the different energies zipping around you all the time, how can you possibly maintain your own psychic space, not get corded, not cord other people, not get stuck in your own or someone else's pictures of who you should be, keep your chakras clean, stay healthy, and in general keep your own psychic integrity balanced?

Stay neutral, and don't resist anything.

Notice now, we didn't say that you have to believe everything you're told (or, in fact, anything you're told), or that you shouldn't have feelings, thoughts, or bodily responses to stimuli. On the contrary, to do so would be to resist having your own impulses, and that is certainly not a neutral position. In Chapter 1 we said that the state of being at one with the universe did not mean having things the way you want them but, rather, having things the way they are.

Having things the way they are means something like saying "yes" to your experience—whatever that may be.

People will be throwing cords at you all the time, and you won't usually be in the kind of meditative posture where you can see them come at you. If you resist the cord, or if you walk around all day judging everyone and comparing yourself to every hound dog who crosses your path, you become sort of psychically solid: You create walls between yourself and others—which is also creating walls between yourself and your experience. Your chakras tighten up. You become a walking tension. And the worst trap of all is to think that you will ever be any way other than that. Resistance, you see, is part of the human condition. So start out by not resisting the fact that you're resistant.

If you have an argument with your boss or spouse or newspaper boy, and that person accuses you of being a stubborn ass, you'll probably want to say, *No, I'm not!* But look at that. Are you not, at that very moment, being a stubborn ass? How much easier to notice that your response is the response of a stubborn ass, and to say, *Yes, that's so, I am a stubborn ass.* And out of your acknowledgment of the truth of the moment, guess what: You're no longer being a stubborn ass.

Now. We did not say that you should go around calling yourself a stubborn ass. If someone says, *You sure are a swell person,* don't say, *No, I'm not, I'm a stubborn ass.* Notice that you probably like being called a swell person, and say, *Thank you.*

When a person communicates with you, he may or may not be saying something you agree with. But in any case, he is another part of the universe—another part of you—

85

and it should be obvious by now that he is giving you an opportunity to find out where you're at by allowing you to have an experience of him.

If you resist your own experience, you get stuck. The point at which you get stuck becomes an incompleted cycle in your life, which you will repeat over and over in varying forms until you allow yourself to have the experience completely. And until you do allow yourself the experience, you will be acting from your resistance to it and from your "pictures."

If you don't recall our discussion of karma in Chapter 1, go back and take another look at it. Karma, we said, is—among other things—acting out of your pictures and incompleted cycles. When you resist your experience you accumulate some karma to deal with later on down the road. If what you're doing is resisting your experience and accumulating karma, do that. Don't resist resisting. But do notice what you're doing, and notice that you are doing it, rather than that It is doing it *to* you. You'll find, sooner or later, that it stops happening—that you stop doing it.

It is axiomatic in psychic development that you become what you resist. The more you resist something, the more attention you have on it all the time, and the more you keep bumping your head against it. If I get angry at you and you resist my anger, (1) I will continue to be angry at you, and (2) you will quickly begin to have feelings of anger yourself. On the other hand, if I get angry at you and you accept my anger, (1) I will deplete my anger almost immediately, and (2) you won't have to bother with the usually unpleasant experience of being angry yourself. This is part of what is meant by loving your brother, turning the other cheek, or coming from a state of love. It is being connected to the universe from your heart chakra.

There are two kinds of exercises you can do to learn about your own resistance and to begin to move out of it. The first exercise is the same kind of sitting meditation you've been doing so far.

1. Sit in the psychic posture, close your eyes, clear your mind, and ground yourself.

2. Starting from your feet and moving up to your head, examine your physical body. See if there's some part that hurts, some part that's stiff, some part that tickles, some part that's going to sleep. Feel the blood rushing around inside you. Feel the psychic energy rushing inside and around you. If something hurts, let it hurt. If something itches, let it itch. Don't resist it, affirm it. If it hurts, pretend that it hurts. If it tickles, pretend that it tickles. You may find the sensation going away and you may not. But don't do anything about it—just notice it.

3. Examine your emotions. What are you feeling? Don't resist it, just feel it.

4. What are you thinking? And what are you thinking about what you're thinking? Don't stop thinking that, affirm it. Think it some more.

5. Where are you? Are you in your body? Are you with your lover from last night? Are you down the block eating an ice cream cone? Be there. When you're where you are, be in the corner of the room. When you're in the corner, be in the center of your head. Welcome home.

6. When you're in the center of your head, come out of your trance.

The second exercise is one you can do anywhere, any time. Let's suppose you meet your friend for coffee, and he has a barrelful of problems which he starts to dump on you: His boyfriend/girlfriend/mother/father/child/dog/auto mechanic doesn't love him, the rent is overdue and he has no money; his parakeet has measles; his waterbed exploded. You'll notice, perhaps, what your first and second chakras feel like. Are you getting tight in the lower abdomen? Or are you getting wide open? What's happening in your fourth chakra? Is your heart opening, or do you feel a tightness in your chest? Where are the cords going?

Pretend that you are made entirely of air and that everything your friend says passes right through you. We are not saying you shouldn't listen and respond where it's appropriate to do so. Just let the charge, the emotional impact, pass through you and neutralize in the air around you. Now notice what's happening in your energy centers. Do this exercise whenever you have a chance to do so.

## Psychic Whacks

No one is grounded and neutral all the time. When you're resisting, as we said, go ahead and resist. You can't get to any new place until you finish being where you are already.

Sometimes, when you're ungrounded, someone will come along and give you a psychic whack. The easiest way to explain being whacked is that it feels like getting bad-vibed or having anger thrown at you. You're crossing the street and some driver has to stop when he doesn't want to. So he thinks you're a bad person, and Whack! you feel guilty for walking across the street. You're in the grocery store and you take the last quart of milk from the shelf, just as someone else who wants milk comes along. That person sees you with the last quart of milk, and Whack! you feel terrible for taking the milk.

Psychic whacks can also take pleasant forms. You're walking in the park and a beautiful woman/handsome man walks past and gives you the eye. Whack! For the rest of the day you imagine what it would be like to spend some time with that person.

What all whacks have in common is that they send you out of your body. They take you away from your experience of the moment and put you into your head. They make you lose track of where you are. They drive you unconscious. They cause you to give up your power to the person who whacked you. And most of all, they're no fun.

There is no particular exercise for dealing with psychic whacks. When you notice you've been whacked, you can run some energy, give yourself a simple healing, or go into your chakras and pull out any cords you may have planted. But the most effective technique is simply to notice that you've been whacked and don't bother whacking the person back. You'll only start a whacky war.

# 4

# PSYCHIC READING

Everyone is psychic, and everyone is a psychic reader—often without realizing it. *You* are a psychic reader. Every time you meet someone and say to yourself, "She seems tired—she looks as though she's had a hard day," or "He seems so changed—he's acting like someone in love," you are doing a psychic reading.

"But that's nothing!" you may say. "Anyone can guess at those things." Indeed, anyone can. But it is more than guessing: It is receiving information about a person without being told.

The examples above are facile—they are examples of undeveloped psychic perception. But these perceptions are easily developed and refined beyond the point of day-to-day intuition. Psychic reading is a skill which, like any other skill, is strengthened and refined through practice and use.

In addition to practice, we suggest you do something else which may sound paradoxical at first: *Learn not to try.*


## Your Life as a Psychic

In order to understand this bizarre instruction, it will help you to understand your life as a psychic thus far. When you pop out of the womb, the "being" we have talked about has recently entered your body. Everything is new, you are wide-open to the world, all your impressions are relatively pure and untainted by memories, experiences, and opinions. You are totally aware and interested. In other words, you are psychic.

Many children, as you can discover by asking them, see colors around people, and put these colors in their drawings. Many children have constant companions in their fairy friends, with whom they talk and play. And, even more often, children are brilliant observers, famous for their tactlessness because they talk about the things we all see but are often too "polite" to say ourselves.

As a child grows older, his parents begin to train him to function in the adult world: "Don't say those things, it's not polite," or "You're too old for fairies," or "That's not true, your aunt *is* a nice lady," or "Those colors aren't real."

As we have talked with them or observed them during readings, we have learned that a great many people were intimidated as children by adults' insistence about what constituted "reality." As children, they were angry that their perceptions of the world were denied, but eventually they gave in—because grown-ups were bigger, because adults' practical knowledge of survival gave them a clear, or at least an apparent, superiority in the world, and because there were too many of them telling children what was or wasn't real. And so, by the time most kids hit puberty, they have either stopped believing in all that stuff, or learned to keep quiet about it.

For many of the people who stopped believing in their own perceptions altogether, the matter became simple. They just don't think about it any more, unless something really strange comes along to shake them up. Some such people, for instance, reenter the psychic world through one dramatic, unexpected experience, such as communicating with a deceased loved one or foreseeing a future event.

Those people who have chosen to keep their perceptions private may continue to have occasional psychic experiences throughout their lives, telling no one for fear they will be laughed at and thought "crazy." Or perhaps they feel free to mention certain small things—to tell a friend, "I somehow knew you would call today"—but not the strange dreams they have, or the voices they hear. Many, many of these people fear that in fact they *are* crazy and are deeply tormented by their worry and self-doubt.

Those people who have never censored their expressions of what they see may be active, practicing psychics or spiritualists, or they may be using their observations and experiences in some other highly creative way. Or, they actually may have been labeled "crazy" and gone into mental hospitals; or they simply may be regarded as cranks and eccentrics. Often, when someone has struggled for years against massive invalidation of his experience, he develops severe, and real, psychic disorders. He may become paranoid, feeling that everyone is out to get him and deny him his experience; he may become schizophrenic, with one half of himself expressing powerful psychic perceptions and intense emotions, and the other half seemingly normal; he may become catatonic and closed off, preferring to live solely in the psychic world in his head rather than battle the opinions and judgments of others.

We are being general in our examples here. Certainly not all cases of mental illness can be traced to repression of the psychic abilities. But very often repression of these abilities leads to repression of emotions, such as anger at being denied free expression, or fear of being punished. These unexpressed emotions can cause physical *or* mental illness. Craziness can also be someone's "act"—his way of presenting himself in the world which distances him from reality and other people, and by which he avoids taking responsibility for his actions.

Now then, back to you. Perhaps the idea of being psychic is totally foreign to you, and you are reading this book because you wonder if even *you* could learn to do it. Or perhaps you've always secretly thought you could do it, but you didn't know how and you thought you were weird. Or maybe you already *know* these things you see and feel are real, and you want to know how to use your abilities to your best advantage, and control them.

## Trying and Not Trying

That gets us back to *not trying.* Trying is a form of resistance. For instance, when you try to be thin you are resisting being fat. Even if you diet and lose 50 pounds, you will continue to think of yourself as fat, or in danger of becoming fat again, and will never allow yourself to have the experience of being thin. All your attention and energy go into the problem of being fat, and you're so focused on your problem that you can never escape it.

Until you have the experience of being fat completely, you never have your own permission to be fat: It's forbidden territory, and so it tempts you. Therefore, you have to be fat over and over, or continuously, before you can escape the endless repetition of being unacceptable to yourself.

On the other hand, if you do not *try* to be thin, you do not have to put psychic energy into the problem of being fat. That is to say, it ceases to be a problem. This process does not guarantee you'll be thin, and it doesn't mean that when you are free of the *need* to be fat you shouldn't diet, if that's appropriate, to lose weight. But the process does free you from your obsession with being fat and establishes the freedom of your own psychic energy in a way that allows you to be *fat or thin,* as you choose. The way out of the trap is to *indulge* yourself in being fat.

"So," you may ask, "how do I indulge myself in being fat?" First of all, stop beating yourself up for being fat. Recognize that being fat is not "bad," it's just what you don't like. The part of you that says being fat is bad is that judge we spoke about earlier, who lives in the back of your mind and is always telling you what's right or wrong, and always passing judgments on the way you and other people are. What you're doing here is coming to recognize your little voice, and to see that it isn't you.

Secondly, ask yourself what it is you get out of being fat, and allow it to be all right with you to want that. For example, you may want attention for being fat. You may think—your little voice may think—that it isn't all right for you to get the kind of attention you get for being fat. Make it all right. Allow it to be.

When it's okay with you to be the way you are, you are free to decide whether or not you want to be that way, and whether or not it's a true expression of *you.* Then you can continue to be fat or become thin, as you wish, without carrying the weighty burden of *having* to be some way that makes you unhappy.

Not trying doesn't mean you shouldn't work to get what you want. Rather, it means don't put your energy into getting what you don't want—being fat—or not getting what you do want—being thin. These are both negative considerations.

The same holds true for psychic work. It doesn't matter where you're coming from in your psychic experience: These abilities are natural, they are part of you, and they are yours to enjoy. It is more a matter of *letting them back in* to your life than trying hard to develop them.

It may be that in the course of your psychic exercises you feel angry, or fearful, or sad. To experience these emotions is okay; you are just recalling the experiences and feelings that at one time you put, or allowed to be put, between you and your psychic-ness. You can cry, yell, simply feel good, or anything else. Whatever happens to you is your road to being psychic. *There is no single right way.*

You do not have to do a detailed psychic reading in order to be an effective healer. In fact, many healers never say a word during their healings. But whether you do verbalize your impressions or not, reading can only help you to be a clear receiving channel for information about your subjects. The more you allow yourself to *know* them—which is all reading really is—the more you can know the nature of their problems and what these problems require to be solved.

Even more simply, reading *is* healing. Many psychics do

not practice the kind of healing we teach in this book, but do give verbal readings. They are just as much healers as those who touch their patients or otherwise work with energy. Amy's experience has shown her that, in fact, certain people are more readily healed by words than techniques. As each client walks in the door, she is able to assess how verbal an approach she will take. For some people, she will explore in her reading the reasons for her client's illness, the function it fulfills in his life, etc. For intellectual people, or people who feel the need to figure things out, this is often the most acceptable approach. Touching their auras and waving her hands would only scare and confuse them, at least in the beginning. Other clients arrive with a great deal of faith in Amy as a healer, and, trusting in her abilities and what they believe to be her unique powers, prefer not to talk about or analyze their ailments.

There are a great many facets to psychic reading, and, as with healing, many styles. Some of the first reading exercises that follow you will be able to do anywhere, by yourself. The next series requires that another person be seated across from you as you read him.

## Pictures and Crazy Pictures

There are many things to look for as you read. As in healing, the aura and the chakras will be your primary sources of information. Psychic information may also come to you in the form of mental images or pictures, which we have discussed throughout this book.

When you read, you may literally *see* a picture. It may loom large on your mental screen, or it may appear in miniature. Such a picture comes from your subject's experience—past, present, or future. For example, you may receive an image of your subject as a small child; or as he appears now, engaged in some activity or with other people; or as he will appear in a few days, months, or years. Images of other people, places, or things may appear to you. All these are pictures which you may merely observe or tell your friend about.

It is tempting to call pictures memories, but that is not really accurate, since they can be images not only from the past but from the present or future as well. Or, you may not *see* pictures at all but, as with auras and chakras, you may simply sense them, or just *know* that they are there.

We use the term "picture" in a broad sense, to describe an image other than just a visual one. A picture may be your own, or it may have been someone else's picture originally, which was handed over to you and which you accepted. For example, you may know someone who thinks he is too skinny, or too fat, or who thinks he has stringy hair, or whatever. You, on the other hand, think he looks just great —and everyone *but* your friend seems to think so. Possibly, somewhere along the line, someone said to him, "Hey, you're skinny." Or, "You're a fattie, why don't you go on a diet?" Or, "Why don't you have thick, wavy hair like your sister's?"

It may never have occurred to your friend that he or she could simply return the picture to its original owner. Your friend is "stuck on a picture." What was originally someone else's image has become his painful reality.

Now, perhaps your friend really does appear to be skinny, or fat, or stringy-haired. He may have started out from the very same place: Someone gave him a picture and he *believed* in it. That is to say, he gave that person power of judgment over him, and the picture became his physical reality.

The same process applies to mental states: People may believe themselves to be stupid, smart, dull, witty, etc., all on the basis of other people's pictures. Even habits may be formed on the basis of a picture. If someone told you, when you were young, that cigarette smoking was "cool," you may have formed an addiction which, at its core, revolves around this other person's pictures. Try this exercise for finding out who gave you your pictures.

### Locating the Source of Your Pictures

1. Ground yourself, and go in to trance.
2. Pick something about yourself that you do not like. Do this exercise with something about your body, or imagine yourself in a situation where you are being dumb, dull, or whatever. This can be a situation you dread occurring, or one from your experience.
3. Watch this picture slowly dissolve. As it disappears, allow other people's faces to appear. These are the original donors of the picture. You may see only one face, you may see several. Dissolve these faces one by one, imagining that you are sending them back to their owners. If you feel angry, or hurt, or anything else as you look at these pictures, go ahead and experience what you're feeling. Tell the people anything you've ever wanted to tell them. If it feels appropriate to you as you dissolve the pictures, forgive the people. If you don't want to forgive them, don't— it isn't time yet. We mention this because when you *are* ready to forgive them for having their pictures, you will be closer to fully forgiving yourself for having whatever prob-

lem you have—fat, skinny, dumb, etc.—, and then you will be that much closer to giving it up. Remember, there is no hurry. If you want to enjoy being hurt or angry or sad for a while, please don't deny yourself this pleasure.

4. Make a picture of yourself and give it some love. Dissolve it.

5. Bring in a big, golden sun of energy, and let it fill your body and aura.

6. Come out of trance.

## Reading Roses

The first basic set of psychic reading exercises is called Reading Roses. We use the simple mock-up of a rose—a symbol of harmony and beauty—to represent the person being read, and a sun—a symbol of abundant energy—to represent his or her personal energy source. A mock-up is a mental model, or image, which you create consciously and intentionally. It differs from a picture or image insofar as these latter models are created unconsciously, or unintentionally. Pictures, etc., may contain all manner of unnecessary and even debilitating energy; a mock-up contains only what you put into it on purpose. The relationship between the rose and the sun represents the relationship between the person and his or her energy.

Rose reading is an excellent way to begin to learn to read, and it is also a very practical method of receiving an overview of someone's development. The rose is merely a symbol. If, as you proceed with the following exercise, you see tulips or petunias or pink elephants, carry on. Whatever works for you is what you should use.

1. Ground yourself, and run energy as shown in Chapter 3 until you feel comfortable.

2. Close your eyes, and imagine a mental picture screen in your head. Imagine yourself gently dusting off the screen with a feather duster. Make a picture of a rose in the center of the screen, and look at all its details—stem, petals, leaves, etc. The rose need not be red, it can be any color you like.

3. Dissolve the rose. Make another rose, more beautiful than the first. Dissolve it. Make another. Dissolve it. Do this five more times; it will give you practice in visualizing. If you can't see the rose on your screen, imagine what one would look like if you could see it.

4. Now make a new rose, and imagine that this rose represents a good friend of yours. What you are doing, in fact, is allowing your friend's energy to fill the rose and transform it. Watch the rose open or close, bloom or wilt, change color or remain exactly the same.

5. Mock up a sun, and put it in the picture. See where it goes in relation to the rose. The sun represents your friend's energy. Is he or she receiving that energy directly? Is the sun bright above the rose, or is it dim? Or does it disappear from the picture altogether? When you have examined this picture to your satisfaction, dissolve it.

6. Repeat this exercise for three more friends or relatives. Repeat this exercise making a rose for Jimmy Carter. You can easily read someone you've never met. Just observe the differences in the roses and their relationships to the suns.

Every picture will have personal meanings for you, so follow your intuition. Amy has her own interpretations: For example, if a rose is brightly colored and blooming directly beneath its sun, the person is in clear communication with his energy source. If the rose is leaning slightly away from the sun, the person is perhaps not willing to really be powerful. If a wilted rose is growing beneath a dim or distant sun, but there is a bud growing on one side of the rose, the person may be giving up an old method of receiving energy, changing old personality traits or ways of being, and allowing a new part of himself to surface. A strong stem may mean that the person is firmly rooted to the Earth, or well grounded.

The color interpretations we suggested in Chapter 1 may help you to understand the colors you see; but first and foremost, if the colors have any special meanings for you, use those to guide you. Be sure that you completely dissolve all your roses when you're finished looking at them.

7. Now make a rose for yourself. If there is anything you don't like about this rose, just change it. Paint it a new color, prune it, or imagine new petals; whatever you wish. Then dissolve the rose.

8. Bring a big golden sun into your body and aura through your seventh chakra, and come out of trance. Congratulations: You have just done six psychic readings.

### How to Read Auras

Reading auras sounds mysterious and difficult, but it is no more difficult than reading roses as you just have done. Remember as you proceed with these exercises that you needn't strain or exert yourself to see auras. Don't try. Relax, and allow the aura to come to you.

When you have practiced rose reading until you feel comfortable with it, continue to use the rose to help you read auras with the following exercise.

1. Make a rose for a friend, just as you did in the previous

exercise, but this time imagine that the rose has a halo: The halo represents the person's aura as the rose represents the person. Start by looking at one color floating around the petals. If you cannot see a color, imagine what the halo would look like if you could see it. Dissolve the rose.

2. Repeat this exercise four times, each time adding a color, until you are up to five colors.

3. Come out of trance. Very good. You've just read an aura.

The next set of exercises is geared toward more advanced reading and will help you further on to use aura reading as an aid in your healing work.

1. Ground yourself and go into trance.

2. Make a picture of a friend of yours. With an imaginary paintbrush, black in the picture until you have a silhouette of your friend.

3. Let your friend's aura fill in around the silhouette, first just as a white halo. Observe where the halo is large and full, where it is thin, or if it stops at some part of the body.

4. Now allow the white halo to become different colors. These are the colors of your friend's aura. If you see one color, that is fine. If you see ten, that is fine also. Probably you will see two or three colors at first, and with practice you will be able to differentiate colors and see auras in more detail. Don't worry about this for the moment, merely watch the colors that you see. Where are they located around the body? Are they static, or do they shift and pulse? Remember, the meanings we ascribed to specific colors in Chapter 1 are just *our* experience of them; follow your own impressions when you can.

5. Dissolve your picture. Choose another friend, and repeat the process. Notice the differences in the two auras. Dissolve this picture.

102

6. Come out of trance, and make your body real. You've just done something very psychic.

## Reading Auras with Your Eyes Open

Clairvoyance, or psychic seeing, which you have just been using, does not of course take place with your physical eyes. It takes place with your psychic eyes. Some people, ourselves included, sometimes see auras with their physical eyes. Amy sees auras in this way when she is particularly relaxed. They usually appear to her as wavy golden halos, although occasionally they will appear as lightly tinted colors. Bill sees them when he looks for them. To him, they frequently appear like Kirlian photographs—a dominant color or colors at the center, with sparks and bursts of energy shooting off into space, or moving around, in other colors.

The fact that Bill sees them when he looks for them, and the fact that Amy sees them when she is relaxed, suggest that the auras are always there—as they are for many children—and the only reason we don't all see them always is that we don't believe we can (see Chapter 7, FAITH, BELIEF SYSTEMS, AND DREAMS).

There is no advantage to seeing auras physically rather than clairvoyantly. In fact, you may see fewer details with your physical eyes than you do with your psychic eyes. But reading auras with your eyes open *is* fun and makes aura reading seem less "imaginary" and more "real."

1. Pick a friend to help you do this exercise. Ask your friend to sit or stand with his or her back to a white wall.

103

A white wall is not necessary but seems to make the exercise easier.

2. Ground yourself. It is not necessary for you to go into trance to see auras in this way. Stand about 20 feet from your friend, and focus on a point in space about four inches above his or her head. Do not focus on the wall or on your friend's face, but rather on the point in space which you have chosen. With practice, you will begin to see your friend's aura. Some people see auras almost out of the corners of their eyes or in their peripheral vision, whereas the auras disappear if they look directly at them.

3. You may practice looking at auras without telling people you are doing so. However, we counsel you to be discreet. It is most disconcerting to have someone gazing at the top of your head or over your shoulder. Early on in her psychic training, Amy made a habit of doing this quite unabashedly, until some of her friends called to her attention that it made them nervous. As you practice, you may find that you can see auras against a background of solid colors other than white, or against any background, or none at all.

## How to Read Chakras

Reading chakras is basically the same as reading auras. However, do not proceed to this exercise until you are comfortable with reading auras, because it is somewhat longer and more strenuous than the previous exercises.

1. Ground yourself and go into trance.

2. Pick a friend and make a silhouette of him in your mind's eye.

3. Focus your attention on the area between the ovaries if your friend is a woman, or at the base of the spine if your friend is a man. Visualize or imagine a disk in this area, observe whether the disk is open or closed, and allow it to fi'l with color.

Remember that you are reading a map. This is the first chakra, and it is concerned with survival. If it is wide open, or the colors are dim or dark, your friend may be having difficulties with some aspect of his survival. If it is closed down, chances are that your friend is not much concerned with his survival at present. If the chakra is green, the color of growth, he may be learning new ways in which to survive. If it is red, the color of feeling, his ability or inability to survive may be an emotionally charged issue. And so on.

4. Proceed, one by one, with each of the seven major chakras, and the hand and feet chakras, reading them in this way. Take your time. It is important that you focus on each chakra separately, one at a time, and not try to look at them all at once yet.

5. After you have looked at each chakra individually, take a look at all of them lined up together. You might imagine yourself stepping back from the picture of your friend, so that you are standing at a greater distance from your picture than you were, and can see all the chakras together. Compare the sizes and shapes of the different energy centers. Which are the largest? Which glow most strongly?

6. Dissolve your picture and come out of trance.

7. Look at your friend's chakras in the same way a day later; a week later. Have they changed in any way?

## Locating Pain in the Aura and Body

This next exercise is of great practical value in healing work. It will give you additional things to work on in a healing, beyond the aura and chakra cleaning you've already learned. First practice this exercise by yourself, as you have practiced the previous reading exercise.

1. Ground yourself and go into trance.

2. Pick a friend and make a silhouette of his or her body in your mind's eye.

3. Postulate that wherever there is a physical pain in your friend's body, a red spot will appear in the picture, encompassing the ailing area. Notice where the spots appear in relation to the chakras. When you have looked at this picture to your satisfaction, dissolve it.

4. Make another silhouette of your friend. Postulate that wherever there is emotional pain red spots will appear in the picture. How do they compare with the first picture? Dissolve your picture.

5. Repeat this exercise using several different friends. Dissolve the pictures when you're finished, and come out of trance.

The next time you do a healing on a friend, do this exercise before the healing. You may tell him what you see or not, as you wish. Your friend may come to you saying, "Ouch! Have I got a headache! Gimme a healing!" When you sit down to do this exercise, you may see a spot of red around and/or in your friend's head. But you may see a much darker and bigger spot of red somewhere else entirely—at the base of his spine, in the pit of his stomach, in his left knee—anywhere. Pay attention to what you see, and don't rule out its validity even if it doesn't make sense to you. *Pain often manifests in an entirely different part of the body than where its source lies.* When you are ready to do your healing, give special attention to all areas which were colored red in your reading.

## Reading and Self-Protection

You may choose to extend your use of psychic reading skills by actually giving readings to people. You may or may not give a reading in combination with a healing, depending upon what seems appropriate in the situation, and what you feel comfortable doing.

We advise you to follow your intuition. As you become accustomed to reading auras and chakras, more sophisticated insights and ways of reading will follow naturally. If you devote time and practice to developing your psychic reading ability, you will find yourself able to answer people's questions about themselves simply by asking yourself the answer.

When you sit down to read a friend, follow the same basic procedure you use in a healing. In this case, seat your friend across from yourself, ground yourself, and ground your friend. Always give yourself a simple cleaning-out before you begin, so that you will be undistracted as you read. Then proceed with "How to Read Auras" and "How to Read Chakras," this time repeating what you observe to your friend.

Actually giving a psychic reading to someone is more fun than looking at him from a distance, but in some ways it is also more difficult. The person you are reading may be scared, nervous, and *very* curious. As a result, he may "get into your head," a phenomenon we mentioned in Chapter

3. He will bombard you with his attention, thoughts, emotions, ideas, and whatever else is floating around in his space. While his intentions may be good, his psychic intrusion may make *you* lose your grounding cord.

The rose, which you learned to use a few pages ago, has another valuable use, as a form of psychic protection against such intrusions.

Simply visualize a rose, as you did in the preceding exercises. Instead of placing it on your mental screen, put it in front of you, just in front of your forehead. Postulate that this rose will be a magnet, catching and absorbing all your readee's cords before they get to you and disrupt your energy. Make another postulate that the rose will remain there, and check it every once in a while as you read. If you suddenly have trouble during your reading you may need to put up a new rose. At the end of your reading, dissolve the rose.

The use of the rose for psychic protection is not limited to giving readings. It is of no end of value in daily life. The next time somebody is getting to you, or you're having an argument, or a psychic "whacky war," try putting up a rose to defuse the situation.

This technique can be a fantastic aid in maintaining your own equilibrium, but even "psychic protection" is not necessary. If you do not resist whoever is getting to you, in a reading or out, you'll find that there is no "you" to get to. The more you can allow all that aggravation and psychic barrage to go right through you, the more effortless you will find your readings and your relationships. Remember, this does not mean you should deny anything you are feeling, but rather that it will not help you to collect the feelings of others in your own psychic space.

## Communication

As you do psychic work of any kind, it is very important to say what you see. In other words, you must find a way to communicate any strong perceptions you have, so that they will not block up inside you and give you a sticky fifth chakra. As you read, you may see something you would not like to say to the person you are reading. Perhaps you are not sure of the information, or you feel that it might make your readee angry, and this frightens you.

Whether you say it *to him* or not is up to you; just be sure you communicate it in some way that takes the charge—the importance—off it for you. This may mean waiting until the person leaves, and saying it to yourself in the mirror. It may mean writing it down. If you feel more comfortable expressing yourself through painting, dance, or some other medium than words, communicate it that way. Whatever works for you will serve as an outlet, just as long as you don't become stuck with the pictures associated with what you've seen.

Some psychics handle difficult information of this sort by telling third parties. Often this approach is quite successful. Sometimes, however, it introduces a whole new problem: dumping.

If you cook a steak for me, and the steak is too rare for my taste, I can tell you that the steak is too rare for me. You then understand that the steak is too rare for my taste—not that it's too rare absolutely; not that you're a bad cook or a bad person, or that I think you're a bad cook or a bad person; not that you did something wrong; only that the steak is too rare for my taste. We have engaged in communication.

If you cook a steak for me, and the steak is too rare for

me, and I go next door and tell John Doe that you don't know how to cook a steak, John Doe's relationship with you is colored by my opinion, which has nothing to do with reality. The relationship the two of you have is damaged. I have a charge on the situation because I have told an untruth to John Doe about you, and *our* relationship will be damaged. John Doe has my picture floating around in his space, and I need him to agree with me about what I've told him, so his and my relationship is damaged. Because all the relationships are damaged, all three of us as individuals are damaged, and, to the degree we use these various pictures in our other communications and our other relationships —consciously or not—we extend the damage far beyond our immediate threesome. This all came about because I engaged in dumping instead of communicating. John Doe, of course, doesn't have to accept what I say as gospel. He can recognize that it is merely an opinion. However, most people do not ordinarily make this distinction. Rather, they often do not distinguish, in their own minds, between fact and opinion. It will help, when you offer an opinion, to identify it as *your* opinion: to say, *"I think* Jane Doe makes the best steaks in Arkansas." It will also help you, in receiving a communication, to recognize the distinction between fact and opinion. Thus, when someone says to you, "Jane Doe makes the best steaks in Arkansas," you will realize that he or she is saying, *"I think . . ."*

Dumping is a lot like gossipping—communicating something which is not neutral to someone who can do nothing about it. The information communicated can be "bad"— Jane Doe doesn't know how to cook a steak—or "good"— Jane Doe makes the best steaks in Arkansas. In either case, the communication is tainted.

110

Opinions, ideas, judgments, evaluations, and the like actually don't need to be communicated at all under most circumstances. They provide no inherent service to you, and none to the world. People, including us, seem to be very fond of communicating such pointless blather, however, since it gets them lots of strokes and agreement about their own superiority. So we do not tell you not to communicate these things; only that, when you communicate that item you saw in your reading to a person other than your readee, don't dump the charge of the item—its psychic or emotional power—on him, and do make sure the charge blows off—dissipates—for you. Otherwise you won't actually have communicated it, and you'll only have to say it again to clear the picture out of your space.

By far the most effective way to handle a communication you don't want to make is to make it anyway. Let us say, for example, that you see something as you read, are confident that it is so, but are afraid it will make your friend angry to hear it. You want to say, "I see that you like being sick— you're getting more attention for that than you have ever gotten from anything else in your life. Unless you're willing to look honestly at this, and choose to get your attention in other ways, I will not be able to heal you."

You have not made a judgment about your friend's condition, but likely you have touched on a sensitive spot, and your friend may angrily deny your observation. If you express the truth as you see it, you may receive an energic zap —previously referred to as a psychic whack. First, it will help you to remember to put up your rose. Secondly, it will help you to remember that no whack can really hurt you unless you are willing to accept it. And finally, if you don't resist your friend's anger, it will go right through you.

111

## Matching Pictures

This brings us back to what is probably the most important aspect of all in psychic work: being in neutral—that is, not becoming emotionally involved with the person you are reading or healing.

It will make things easier for both of you if you ask your friend not to meditate or go into trance with you. Frequently people think they will facilitate the reading or healing by meditating with you as you work. This is not so. For one thing, people meditate in different ways and may find it difficult to pay attention and listen to you if they are off in their heads or on cloud nine. You want them to be right *here.*

More importantly, as you go into trance you are resonating at your own energy level. If your friend meditates with you, he may naturally, without realizing it, go right along with you as you trance. He can thereby defeat one of the main purposes of going into trance in the first place, which is to raise your energy level high enough above that of your readee to ensure that you remain emotionally separate from him during the reading or healing.

If the two of you are at the same energy level, you may "match pictures" with your friend. This means that observing certain of your friend's experiences summons up similar experiences of your own. Your memories may in turn summon up intense feelings which will clutter your mind and thus clutter your reading. This is a very important concept: Matching pictures is usually the cause of the sudden feeling that you can't see a thing during a reading.

Here is a simple example of matching pictures: You are buzzing along, happily reading your friend's aura, when you see a spot of dark red. As you tell your friend that this spot looks like anger in his aura, you begin to feel very uncomfortable, nervous, and confused. If you are a practiced clairvoyant, you may be able to see actual images, or pictures, in your friend's aura. Or you may sense them. Or, most likely, you will only know that suddenly you are very ill-at-ease.

It may have happened that your friend's mommy spanked him when he was five, and he never forgave her for it. Perhaps your mommy spanked you when *you* were five, and it is still, so to speak, a sensitive area. While you were not in neutral above your friend's energy level, you bumped into a matching picture and got stuck. Your body's memory of your experience has been triggered by his similar one, and all you can focus on is your spanking, *whether you are conscious of it or not.*

Don't despair. Anyone can match a picture, and it is not difficult to remedy the problem. First say to your friend, "Excuse me a moment, I need to make some adjustments in my trance," or "Just a minute while I scratch an itch in my seventh chakra," or some-such. Step back in your head, reground yourself, and raise your energy level by running more Earth and cosmic energy through your body. If you are at a higher energy level, you will be better able to *observe* matching pictures without *feeling* them. Next, reground your friend.

If you have an idea of what your matching picture is, place it on your mental screen and dissolve it. It might be anything: You both had traumatic adolescent acne; you both have jealous boyfriends or girlfriends, premature ejaculations, a fear of heights, etc., etc., etc. You can also get stuck on a powerfully happy or positive picture, although it is less noticeable and less bothersome in a reading.

If you cannot see the picture clearly, sit back and let whatever imagery comes along fill your mind. If you receive something, no matter how unexpected, dissolve the imagery. If you receive nothing, dissolve *that*. If dissolving the picture doesn't seem to help, imagine that the unpleasant feeling you are having is a big blob of energy, any color you choose. Put it on your mental screen and dissolve it.

Next, close down your second chakra halfway. This will further separate you from your friend.

Then think of five ways in which you and your friend are not alike: He has brown hair, you have blond hair; she is a school teacher, you are a milkman; he likes okra, you don't; she is twenty-seven, you are thirty-four; you think psychic stuff is voodoo, your friend doesn't. This technique may sound simple, but you won't appreciate its potency until you try it. *You are not your friend.* You must look at all his or her games and troubles and say: This is not my problem.

Even though it sounds like nothing but a headache, the experience of matching pictures can be of tremendous value to you. It can point out to you those areas in which *you* have stored or blocked-up energy and feelings, and help you to release it by making you aware of it.

One of our teachers, Lewis Bostwick, was in the habit of advising his students, who were soon to become professional readers: "Don't forget that your clients shouldn't be paying *you*, you should be paying *them*. You get to look at all your grundgy pictures and get rid of 'em."

So, to recap—when you get stuck on a picture in a reading:

1. Reground yourself and your friend.
2. Raise your energy level above his by running more energy.

3. Dissolve any pictures you may have.
4. Put up a new rose.
5. Close down your second chakra.
6. Think of five ways in which you are different from your friend.

Another problem which plagues beginning psychic readers is seeing too many things at once. What with auras, chakras, cords, pictures, spirit guides, and symbols of past lives (these will be discussed in Chapter 8), sometimes the beginner isn't sure exactly *what* he is seeing. You can solve or prevent this problem by deciding in advance what you are going to look at—aura, chakras, cords, whatever. Focus totally on the area of your choice, give it your complete attention. You can move on to another area when you're through with the first.

**Paying Attention**

This brings us to what the Tibetan Buddhists call *one-pointedness,* or what we Westerners call *paying attention.* We touched on this subject in Chapter 3, and it's time to take a different kind of look at it.

Paying attention is central to psychic success. "Of course I pay attention!" you may say. But look again. Observe yourself to see how easily your mind will wander as you do a healing, give a reading, or go about your daily business.

B., a client of Amy's, complained of being overweight. No matter what she did, she couldn't take off the twenty pounds that made her feel ugly and uncomfortable. Amy gave her a homework assignment: to eat. To really *eat.*

115

"Oh, no!" said B., "I tried that once! I gave myself permission to eat everything that I wasn't allowed to eat, everything I wanted . . . and I gained twenty pounds in two weeks!"

Amy explained to her that deciding to eat everything that had been forbidden was just the other side of worrying about all the things she couldn't have. What was keeping her from losing weight was that she never really paid attention, while she ate, to simply eating. If she ate a piece of cake, she worried about the calories and lack of nutrition. If she ate a salad, she lauded herself for a dietetic and healthful choice. She was always eating before a jury of one: herself. And since most of the time her eating was an offense punishable by self-hate and feeling bad, eating with relish and enjoyment was usually something she was not allowed to do.

As we all know so well, whatever is forbidden is most tempting. While the cookies are on the top shelf, they are impossible to resist. And so, B.'s homework was to return to eating—to just sit and eat, paying full attention to the food, without guilt or judgment.

She called Amy the next day to say, "I've discovered that what I really enjoy is the *tasting.* So every time I walk past some food, I have a mouthful of it. Instead of rushing to eat and get it over with because it's bad to be eating, I slowly taste it. And I find that one bite or two is enough."

Another client of Amy's worried about his cigarette smoking. "I don't think it's good for me," he said. "What can I do?" The look in his eyes was unmistakable. He secretly hoped that Amy, his psychic, would tell him to quit. If it was bad for him, she would know; and if he continued against her instructions, he was *really* a failure.

116

Amy said, "I'm not going to tell you to quit or to smoke. Do what you want, it doesn't make any difference to me. All I ask is that you *pay attention* before, during, and after you smoke. Watch how you feel. If you don't enjoy it, don't do it. If you do enjoy it, have fun. At the moment, you don't even know yourself whether you like it or not, because you're not really smoking. Instead, you're worrying about whether it is right or wrong, healthful or debilitating. You don't have time for real satisfaction or lack of it, which should be your guide to whether or not you smoke."

Fixing your attention on one point is the most efficient way to find out what you really want or don't want, like or dislike. Then you have the freedom to choose what you really want.

In psychic reading, one-pointedness is equally valuable. Any information in the universe is available to you —you can know anything. And in a reading, you can know anything at all about a person, provided there is some agreement between the two of you that you should know it.

Let us say, for example, a friend you are reading asks you a question. Your ability to receive the answer depends on your ability to focus fully on that question. If you are afraid to answer the question, or if you are afraid that you might in fact be powerful enough to *know* the answer, your mind may stray. You may become confused, bored, or sleepy. You may start thinking about the movie you saw last night, or what you're going to have for lunch. Slow down, and ask yourself what is between you and the information. If you continue not to be comfortable answering, you may simply say so to the person you are reading. You are not even obliged to give a reason.

117

## Getting on with It

Occasionally you will run into someone who, although he has come to you for a reading, does not really want you to look at him psychically. Just as you cannot heal someone against his will, neither can you look at him against his will. Amy experiences this situation as if the information is blocked: She just isn't getting anything, even after using all the separation and neutrality techniques she knows. And while it is not easy for her to do, she says, "Is it true that you don't want me to see you? I can't read you unless you want me to." More often than not, despite his or her discomfort, the person is willing to admit that the answer is "yes."

This is an appropriate place to mention that in all areas of psychic work involving you and another person, it will not help you to be pushy. Let it be known among your friends that you would like to practice the psychic techniques you are learning from this book. The ideal situation is to let them come to you. However, if it is more appropriate to ask, ask gently, and give your friends room to say "no."

"Psychic" is a scary word to many people, some of whom you would least expect to be scared by it. Amy had many surprises when she was beginning work. Often the friends who seemed to have the most liberal attitudes and philosophies were the most critical and frightened. Conversely, people who had never expressed an interest in ESP or meditation or the like were curious and helpful. We can assure you that, as time passes, you will know immediately who will be scared and who won't. Meanwhile, be considerate, and remember how you felt about the subject several years ago, or even as you began reading this book.

Lewis Bostwick, whom we mentioned earlier, was also in the habit of saying, "Give your readees just a little more than they can have." That cryptic advice becomes crystal clear the more practice you have with reading, and is equally applicable to healing.

"Havingness" means, in this context, how much growth or healing or information about yourself you are willing to receive at a given time. Havingness in general means what you are willing to give yourself. For example, if money is important to you, do you have the havingness to make as much as you want? Does your havingness extend to $100? $1,000? $1,000,000? If love is important to you, do you have the havingness to have a successful love affair or marriage?

Many people do not have a very high havingness level. When receiving a reading, the amount of information which you are willing to hear and pay attention to and think about is your level of havingness. In a healing, the amount of healing energy which you are able to take into your body in order to transform it is your havingness level.

Lewis advises giving your readees a little extra because the information sinks in somehow, even if it is not on a conscious level right away. Many is the time we have received phone calls from people we read or advised six months or a year earlier, telling us, "Wow, was I ever mad when you told me such-and-such, but it sure makes sense now! I just didn't understand what you *meant* by blahblah-blah until last week, when it all clicked." On the other hand, if you give the person you are reading too much at once, you may so totally alienate him that it will take him ten lifetimes to begin to hear what you said.

Psychic reading is more than a service to others; it is a service to yourself. As you see your matching pictures and

119

discover those things that can stick you, you are able to take the charge off them by dissolving your pictures. And you are able to relocate your own, personal space by saying, "I am not my friend, I am myself." For Amy, learning to read has had another value. It forced her to have strong opinions, to take a firm stand and stick by it, which was previously difficult for her to do.

Now, at the risk of seeming confusing, the greatest thing of all about reading appears at first glance to be the exact opposite of what we just told you. As another psychic reader said to Amy, "The great enlightenment is *I am he.*" The more you read (and, we trust, the more you *live*), the clearer it becomes that you are everyone, and everyone has the same problems you have. What you are really doing as you read is talking to yourself, about yourself. What could be simpler?

# 5

## SOME ADVANCED HEALING AND READING TECHNIQUES

The exercises in this chapter are more advanced than those you have done previously. As with all the exercises in this book, do not hurry yourself. You are receiving a full psychic course in nine chapters, and it is better to repeat an exercise until you feel comfortable with it than to rush through the book.

Remember, too, that it is all right if some of the exercises in this chapter are easier for you than previous ones were. Just because the exercises appear in a certain order in this book does not mean they will be progressively more difficult for you. Spend time on those you need to spend time on, and don't compare your progress with someone else's progress, or with the progress you think you're supposed to make. Each person is different and will go at his or her own pace.

## Cleaning the Chakras

Cleaning the chakras can give some of the most dramatic results of all the psychic techniques, both in healing others and in healing yourself. Here is the method for cleaning your own chakras.

1. Ground yourself and go into trance.

2. Be in your third chakra. Imagine that any unsavory energy, pictures, or clutter of any kind which is stored there will be flushed down from your third chakra to your second, where it will collect any stuff in that chakra, and then down to your first, repeating the process. Flush whatever you collect in these chakras down your grounding cord and into the Earth. It is not necessary to examine what you are removing as you do this exercise, although you certainly may do so.

3. Be in your fourth chakra, and repeat this process in reverse. Pull any accumulated psychic goo up from the fourth chakra to the fifth, sixth, and seventh, and send it out your seventh chakra. Imagine it being pulled outside your aura, where it will dissolve into neutral energy.

4. Now, be in your first chakra. Fill this center with clean, orange energy, and imagine it swirling and glowing throughout the chakra. You have just removed the clutter. Always fill up a space which you have cleaned out by adding clean energy. Nature abhors a vacuum in psychic space no less than in physical space; if you leave your space empty, there's no telling what will collect in it.

5. Repeat step 4 in the second and third chakras. Then close each of the three lower chakras to a comfortable degree.

6. Fill the four upper chakras with orange energy, one by one. As you learned in "Color Meditation," in Chapter 3,

orange is always an effective color, but if it is your sense that you would like to use a different one, go ahead. Do not close down the upper four chakras.

7. Come out of trance.

Cleaning chakras is an adaptable technique. You can do it as much or as little as you like, depending on how thorough a healing you want to give yourself, or how much time you have. If you are feeling ambitious, after step 6 you can also remove cords and look for sticky pictures that are inhibiting your energy flow.

To heal another person by this method, ground yourself and your friend, then hold your hand over his third chakra and imagine that it is pushing the crud down through the lower chakras into his grounding cord, and thence into the Earth.

Next, hold your hand over your friend's seventh chakra, and imagine that you are pulling the junk from his fourth chakra up through his upper chakras, collecting all the unwanted stuff on the way. Pull it up and out of his seventh chakra, and conclude by filling each chakra with fresh energy.

## Aligning the Chakras

Each chakra is connected by a small energy-stem to a main energy channel which runs behind and parallel to the spine in the energy body. Sometimes a physical ailment occurs in conjunction with a particular chakra becoming disconnected from the energy channel, or becoming tilted out of alignment with it. Sometimes pictures from past or future lives, or pictures having to do with experiences in this lifetime which a person has not released, will become lodged in a chakra and distort its energy. Once you have cleaned out your chakras, or those of your friend, you can take a look at the main energy channel and examine the various chakras' relationships to it. A healer frequently can accomplish a great deal simply by straightening out chakras which have fallen out of alignment and connecting those which have become disconnected.

To do this exercise, ground yourself and go into trance, then clean the chakras as you did in the preceding exercise. Next, beginning with the first chakra and moving up through the seventh—completing your work on one chakra before moving on to the next—picture the chakra's stem with the energy channel running behind it. Is the stem connected firmly with the channel? If the connection is loose, picture yourself tightening it as you would tighten a lightbulb in a socket. If it is disconnected, simply hook it up again.

When you're sure that all the chakras are connected with the energy channel, return to the first chakra. Imagine that as you look into it you are looking directly into the bell of a flower. If the bell is tilted in any way such that you are not looking at it eyeball to stamen, grip it firmly but gently with your psychic fingers and straighten it out. Do the same for all the remaining chakras. Then bring in a huge golden sun through your seventh chakra and let its energy filter down your energy channel, or that of the person you're reading, spreading its light throughout the energy body and running out the grounding cord. Come out of trance.

## Owning Your Body

Earlier on, in Chapter 3, we suggested that you talk to your body. Here is another exercise that may seem peculiar at first. It is designed to reacquaint you with your body, to reestablish you as the owner of your physical space, and to remind you that, despite anything anyone's chattering mind might say to the contrary, this is *your* body.

To "own" something, in psychic lingo, is to make it completely yours. For example, your parents taught you to walk, so they may still own part of your legs, and you may never have fully owned them yourself. You may have grown up believing your genitals were somehow unclean, and you may never have really owned them and occupied them as your own.

Areas of your body which you have not owned are areas in which blocks may occur when you try to run Earth and cosmic energy through them. They are areas in which you will be unconscious or "asleep" most often, and they are areas in which physical maladies are most likely to occur. Your aura around these areas may be wispy or virtually nonexistent.

You are the king or queen of the castle which is your body. To take control of your domain, begin by grounding yourself. Then, be in your toes—which is the same thing as being in the center of your head, or being in the corner of the room, or being in any of your chakras, except you're in your toes. Put *all* your awareness in your toes. You probably don't think of your toes too often, so take your time and find out how they feel, and how you feel being there.

Next, be in your feet. Are they light, heavy, tingly, achey? Be in your calves.

One by one, be in every part of your body. Notice that

you don't have to *move* from one part to another, you can simply *be* in one part and then *be* in another. Be in your knees, thighs, buttocks, genitals, hips, stomach, chest, shoulders, upper arms, elbows, forearms, hands, fingers; be in your lower back, upper back, neck, chin, lips, tongue, teeth, nose, cheeks, eyes, ears, hair, head. Spend as much time as you wish in each place, and feel free to visit other parts of your body that we have left out of our list.

As you enter each part of your body, talk to it. Say hello to your stomach, and ask it if there are any home improvements it would like you to make. It might say, "Not so heavy on the Mexican food," or "Open your belt another notch." Talk to your feet. They may say, "Don't take me for granted, I want softer shoes," or "Thanks for the Epsom salts."

You may find that in some parts of your body you feel pleasant and comfortable, while in others you become bored, or heavy, or tense. These latter are likely to be those areas which you have not fully owned.

As you visit each part of your body, be aware of your sensations, both pleasant and unpleasant. The first step in feeling that your entire body belongs to you is noticing where you feel at home and which parts you are estranged from. Look and see if you are storing any painful pictures in your estranged parts. If so, return these pictures to their rightful owners, as you learned to do in Chapter 4.

When you finish owning your body, return to the center of your head. From here, make a picture of your body on your mental screen. Give this picture lots of love and appreciation. Dissolve the picture and come out of trance.

**Being Well**

Since healing implies that something needs repair, healers tend to focus on what's "wrong" with a physical or psychic body, rather than what's "right" with it. Yet, this focus is a little misleading. Healing is not so much the process of correcting that which isn't working as it is the process of allowing to work that which is natural.

In Chapter 4 we talked about "not trying"; we said that healing abilities are natural and that using these abilities is more a matter of letting them back in to your life than trying hard to develop them.

By and large, the exercises in this book are designed to allow your natural state of power and wellness to return to your control. They are designed to *unteach* you some of the patterns you learned as a child, which were useful in surviving as a child but which are not especially appropriate now, and may even be debilitating. Asthma, for instance, may have gotten you a lot of parental attention when you were young. But is that the sort of attention you want *now?* Is getting attention worth not being able to breathe?

What follows is an exercise to put you in touch with what already works, and to bring the rest of your energy into alignment with that.

1. Ground yourself and go into trance.

2. Look at your aura for spots that are radiant with healthy, vibrant, clean, golden energy.

3. Raise the energy in the rest of your body to match the high energy of those healthy spots. Again, what you are doing is postulating that the energy will rise when you tell it to; then you are allowing it to rise as high as it wants to.

4. Circulate the energy through your chakras and aura, then bend over and come out of trance.

You can apply this exercise to healing others simply by looking at their auras for healthy spots, instead of looking at your own. Then raise their energies as you raised your own.

## Letting Go of Illness

The previous exercise will give you a good bead on your havingness level, among other things. If you go into trance and all you see is gray energy, ask yourself how high you're willing to be, and ask for the answer to appear as a color. Take that color—whatever it is—and bring it down through your seventh chakra into your third. Then match the rest of your energy to that energy, and finish with step 4 of the exercise. Do the exercise again the next day. Your energy will probably be somewhat higher than it was. Whatever color your energy is raise it to the next highest color— whatever that is for you—before moving on to steps 3 and 4. See how many days you have to do the exercise before gold appears in your aura.

Being well is essentially a matter of allowing yourself to be in that condition. Sometimes you will not allow yourself to be well. Both Amy and Bill have, from time to time, gotten ill simply in order to get a vacation, or some sympathy. Being ill is not as pleasant or as easy a way to get what you want as simply *asking* for sympathy or *taking* a vacation. It works, up to a point, but it is rarely the most satisfying way to handle your desires.

If you have an ailment you want to get rid of, just let go of it. *Getting rid* of something is an active approach which requires putting energy into the ailment. *Letting go* of it is as easy as opening your psychic hand.

1. Ground yourself and go into trance.

2. Locate the red spots in your aura that represent your illness. The spots may be some color other than red—just ask to see your illness, and the spots will appear in their appropriate colors.

3. Fill each spot with helium.

4. Let each helium-filled spot float, like a balloon, up and out of your aura, into space where it will neutralize.

5. Bring clean, golden energy in through your seventh chakra and let it fill all the spaces where your spots were.

6. Come out of trance.

## Your Inner Voice

The following exercise is one of the simplest in this book, yet we find that it brings results in all areas of psychic work.

Earlier on, we referred to the *inner voice*—that part of you which already knows everything, and which supplies those answers to your questions which will best aid you. To get in contact with this voice, first close your eyes and ground yourself. Think of a question you would like to ask, such as, "Do I really want to go to the prom with Eddie?" or "Is my boss planning to give me a raise?" or "Does my sister really like okra?"

On your mental screen print a big YES. Next to that, print a big NO. Ask your question, and see which word lights up. We know this sounds too easy, but life *doesn't* have to be hard. Try it. You may be surprised at how quickly and easily you get an accurate answer.

This technique is also useful in talking to your body. For example, Amy sometimes checks out her nutritional balance this way. "Hey, body," she will say, "do you want more vitamins?" If she receives a "Yes," she will go down the list of vitamins—A,B,C,D,E, etc.—receiving a "Yes" or "No" for each.

You can vary this technique as much as you wish by adding "sometimes," or "a little bit," or "a lot," or any other gradation of answer. Be as specific as you want.

## Advanced Absent Healing and Self-Healing

In Chapter 4 we showed you how to read illness in the body. To do the following absent healing exercise, go through step 3 of "Locating Pain in the Aura and Body," finding the red spots in your picture of your friend. For the moment, ignore his or her chakras.

When you have located the painful areas, pick one of them and imagine a glowing orange ball in the center of it. Imagine this ball slowly filling the spot of red until there is no red left. Do this with each red spot. If some spots will not turn orange, repeat the exercise. If they remain red, probably your friend will not allow these areas to be healed. Recall our discussion of "havingness" in Chapter 4; allow your friend to have only as much healing as he can accept comfortably at this time.

Repeat this exercise, reading and healing the chakras rather than the body.

Finally, make a picture of yourself and do this exercise, first with your body and then with your chakras. Always dissolve your pictures at the end of an exercise. While this healing method is primarily intended for use in absent or self-healings, it is occasionally useful in working with someone seated across from you. For instance, if for some reason he is uncomfortable having you move your hands in his aura, you can heal him with this technique.

# 6

## WHY DO
## PEOPLE GET SICK?

Most of us think that getting sick is something unlucky which befalls us, an accident in which we have no hand. Perhaps we feel we got sick because we went out in the rain without a hat on, or because there was a bug in the air. Then why do some people live healthy, hatless lives, and not others? Why are some people always down with a bug?

**What Do You Get out of Being Sick?**

Getting sick is not an accident at all. Being sick has a lot of payoffs. A payoff is what you get out of something. It may be pleasant, like love, and you may wish to keep it. Or it may be unpleasant, like pain, and you may wish to be rid of it. In either case it is what the mind thinks it needs to

132

survive. When you notice what you get out of something—
when you discover what the payoff is for you—you begin to
know what your mind believes you need, and you mark the
first stages of liberation from your personal belief system.

We can recognize some payoffs easily; others are harder
to see. For instance, if you are confined to bed, you not only
can get a lot of sympathy and attention, you can also have
people wait on you, clean up after you, and be nicer to you
than they might ordinarily be. You can also miss that important meeting you don't want to attend, or miss the week-
end visit to your in-laws, or blame your illness on the food
you ate at the restaurant you didn't want to go to but which
your husband or wife insisted on trying.

Several doctors we know agree that most of the ailments
their patients bring them are psychosomatic in origin—that
is, they have no organic bases. Nothing is wrong with their
patients' bodies, but the patients have *decided* that something is or should be wrong, and begin to have all the
symptoms of an illness. If the doctors tell their patients,
"Look, there's nothing wrong with you, you're as healthy
as a horse. Why don't you go see a movie and get back to
your life," the patients simply go find a new doctor who will
be sympathetic to their complaints. As a result, some doctors have learned to turn an understanding ear to their
patients and then give them placebo medication—sugar
pills or some other harmless substance. The patients can
then imagine that the sickness they've created in their own
minds is being treated by expert medical care. Soon
enough, the attention these patients get from their doctors
satisfies their needs, and they get back on their feet again,
never fully realizing that they've been treated like children
and babied back into accepting the health they never really
lost.

In healing yourself or your friends, it will help you to

recognize the enormous power of the mind to create apparent illness where none really exists. The fact that such illnesses are creatures of the imagination does not lessen their power in the lives of the victims: People can die from imagined illnesses. Just as we can use our minds to create headaches, colds, or fevers, we can also use our minds to create really serious biological problems such as ulcers, heart attacks, and cancer. Of course, the illness the mind creates it can also cure—which is, in part, what this book is about.

As we mentioned earlier, a great deal of illness is attributed to "germs." While it is technically true that a germ will act out its cycle in a body, there is still the question of why sickness happens at some times rather than others, and to some people more than to others. Since there are germs around us all the time, in a reading the psychic looks for the reasons why the germs are activated in the body.

To talk for a moment on a purely physical level, illness is a cleaning-out process for the body. Rather than looking at a cold as a bunch of unpleasant symptoms that *happen,* it can be looked at as a way of expelling poisons. The body "runs a fever" and then breaks into a sweat in order to expel poisons through the skin. A runny nose is the body's way of expelling poisons through the mucous membranes. Diarrhea is the body cleansing itself through its excretions.

These poisons are likely to be accumulated from drinking, smoking, eating junk food or too much food, taking pills and drugs, or pollution. Viewing sickness from this angle, it is not so much a bad thing as a statement on the body's part that it is time to clean house. In fact, if the body cleans house every now and then, it will prevent the buildup of poisons which can lead to much bigger and more painful diseases than a cold. Sickness can actually be an active, positive choice on the road to health and happiness.

As we've mentioned before, both Amy and Bill occasionally get ill simply in order to take a vacation. When we've been working hard for long periods of time and not receiving the love and support we want from our friends and families; when we've promised ourselves a vacation but never quite get around to taking it; when we have something to do we'd rather avoid; when we just want to lie around in bed for a day or two and aren't willing to simply say so—all these are times when the symptoms of illness have appeared just strongly enough to persuade us that we must cancel all our appointments and lounge around eating soup and boxes of candy, and watching a lot of television. It's clear, though, that this way of taking time out is neither as effective nor as satisfying as saying, "I want some attention," or "I've been working too hard and I'm taking two days off to go to the beach." Payoffs have a way of exacting a price, such as *having* to spend two days in bed when you'd really rather be at the beach, or making people stop inviting you to go places if you always get sick at the last minute anyway.

## Being Sick Is Not "Bad"

In order to know *why* a person has gotten sick, it invariably helps to know *what* that person is getting out of his or her illness. As may be apparent by now, "getting something" does not necessarily mean getting something we ordinarily regard as "good." But when you can find out what someone gets from his illness—whatever it may be—

you'll be well on the way to helping him to help himself recover.

All this is not to suggest that it is "bad" to be sick. There's nothing wrong with being sick—it's just the other side of being well, except it usually doesn't feel as good.

In Chapter 3 we said that illness is a process by which your body communicates information to you about imbalances and disruptions you are making, or allowing to be made, in your life. While such imbalances may be as simple as not taking a needed break from your daily routine, they can be much more complicated. For example, if you have heart trouble, your body might be telling you that you're eating too much cholesterol.

When you do a psychic reading or healing, part of what you're doing is discovering imbalances in your friend's total life-force and helping him to see what he is doing, and what results he is getting. When you communicate your discoveries to your friend, he has the chance to make a choice about whether he wants what he's getting out of his illness, or would rather have something else, or can get what he wants more directly.

Frequently, an ill person's message to those close to him is, "I'm going to punish you for not loving me enough—see, you've made me sick," or "You haven't noticed that I need love from you, so I'm going to be sick and then you will have to give it to me." A person is expressing his needs and desires through his most fundamental tool—his body.

Particularly in the case of a lingering or chronic illness, a "nurse" may develop hostilities toward an ill mate or friend to whom he or she is constantly giving time and attention, receiving little in return. Time and time again we have seen the friends of chronically ill people insist staunchly that they are nothing but sorry for their friends, then finally admit that they are hurt and furious. Being angry or frustrated over another's illness is one of the greatest taboos we have in this culture.

Underlying feelings of resentment can result in some very bad feelings. Knowing, consciously or unconsciously, that the best way to get attention from someone is to be sick, the ill person may prolong his illness. Or, he may recover, then lose the attention he was getting, feel frustrated, and become sick again in order to repeat the cycle.

Two of the most popular times for people to get sick are (1) when they are on the verge of, or in the midst of, major change, and (2) when things are going exceptionally well for them.

Change, as we said in Chapter 3, drives the mind into survival. When you alter, or prepare to alter, a pattern of your behavior, your mind feels threatened. When a minor change is on your horizon, you may find yourself slicing your thumb instead of an onion, locking yourself out of your house, or catching a slight cold. When a major change is coming up, your mind may go to greater extremes to prevent it: You may fall down and break a leg, your car may be stolen, or you may have a fight with your spouse, professional colleagues, or best friend.

In the same way, when everything is working in your life, your mind may react out of your childhood pictures and decide that you really don't deserve all the goodies that are falling into your lap. It's hard to enjoy a success, no matter how marvelous, with a temperature of 103 degrees. Thus, if you get ill at such a time, you are cutting yourself off from the happiness you don't feel you deserve. If you just got a raise, your friend who owns a house in the Bahamas asks if you would like to use it during your winter vacation, your children are all on the honor roll at school, and your favorite stock just went up 50 points, you may find the same sorts of things happening that happen during change periods in your life.

Now, we don't mean to suggest that the *only* times you get sick are times of upheaval, or that every change in your life will produce an illness. Not at all. In fact, during certain times of change and stress you may find that you absolutely control your physical well-being. If you feel as if you're getting the flu, but you have a meeting to attend that's extremely important to you, you may find that you put off your illness until the meeting is over. Many people we know have had such experiences. Bill, in fact, used to play a little game with himself about it.

For about a year, every so often Bill would feel a cold coming on, or feel his back going out just when an important job was coming due. He began to make agreements with his body that ran something like this: *Listen, pal,* Bill would say to his body, *I feel that you want to get sick, and it seems to me that what's happening is you're under pressure and in fear about this job. But it's very important to me to get the job done well and on time, and I really can't afford to get sick now. Let's make a deal. You won't get sick on me until the job is over, and I promise you a two-day vacation as soon as it's done.*

Then Bill would write his own name in on his calendar for the first two open days after the job was due and go back to work. He would not get sick, at least until the job was over, and by then he'd be on his days off and his body usually found it would rather spend those two days playing than lying in bed with a fever and runny nose—so often, he wouldn't get sick at all.

Basically, life is a kind of game in which you can have a good time or not, as you choose. But in any case, the game will go on for you until you die. Since your body will be dead a long time, and alive for only a comparatively short time, you might as well enjoy the game as not.

Some people actually enjoy being sick. They like to manipulate others, and they like the kinds of attention they get when they appear to be helpless. They like hanging out in bed for weeks or months on end, and they like being free of the responsibilities of life. Such people may even come down with long-term, chronic ailments which a doctor might or might not be able to diagnose. It is possible for a person to be "ill" in this way consciously, knowing exactly what he or she is doing, and knowing exactly what he or she is getting out of the situation, but it isn't likely. Much more often a person in such a situation truly believes he or she is sick and believes he simply *can't* (as opposed to *won't*) cope with the problems of daily life. If this is your idea of a good time, and if you can get the people around you to play this version of the game with you, why then, enjoy it! But if lying around in your pajamas watching twenty years' worth of daytime television and eating endless bowls of chicken soup sounds as if it could get a bit tedious, you might want to choose a different way to play the game of your life.

### You Get What You Ask For

Ultimately, you get exactly what you want—although the level at which you want it may be an unconscious one. If you start to feel queasy every time you have to clean the bathroom, you may think you don't want to feel queasy, but the fact of the matter is that you *do* want *not* to clean the bathroom, and feeling queasy may be a way out of doing it, or at least a way to get sympathy in the context of cleaning the bathroom. You may not even really care about cleaning the bathroom; you may just use it as a way of getting sympathy.

Nine out of ten times we do healings we find that our clients are getting something out of their ailments that they either didn't recognize they were getting or thought was a by-product of their illnesses. Simply discovering what the payoff is, and discovering how important it is to them, almost always clears up the ailment. If you or a friend of yours have some illness, one of the things you're going to want to do in the course of your psychic healing is to find out what it is the person is getting out of that condition. Another thing you're going to want to know is whether he is willing to "let go" of the illness.

Letting go of the illness means that you are willing not to have it any longer. It does not mean that you want it or don't want it. We assume that at a conscious level you don't want to be sick. But letting go of an illness means being willing to do without the payoff as well, or to get the payoff in some other form.

If you don't want to clean the bathroom and you get queasy every time you have to do it, probably you're willing not to feel queasy. But are you willing to clean the bathroom *and* not feel queasy? Are you willing to do without your payoff—let's say it's sympathy for feeling queasy—or get it in some other way? Are you willing, for instance, to say to the person you live with, or to your friend, "I know I have to clean the bathroom, but I really hate doing it, and every time I have to do it I start feeling sick to my stomach. I want some sympathy because I have to do something I hate doing. Will you please give me five minutes of sympathy?"

You may find that by getting your sympathy out in front,

you can go ahead and clean the bathroom without feeling queasy. In fact, you may find that just by telling the truth about it you can clean the bathroom without getting queasy even if your friend says, "Sorry, I'd love to give you some sympathy, but I'm late for my appointment at the hairdresser's." Ultimately you can let go of an illness without all the preamble. Letting go of an illness is as easy as letting go of this book is in the physical world: Just open your psychic hand.

Being able to let go of an illness is very similar to owning your body, as we discussed in Chapter 5. When you own a thing, you can do what you want with it. You can keep it, let it go, put it on a shelf to play with on rainy days. When a thing owns you, you have to do what *it* wants. If an illness owns you and it wants you sick in bed, guess where you'll go?

In a way, having an illness is a little bit like having your house haunted. In your own space—physical or psychic— you are the most important being (in *or* out of a body) there is, and what you say is the law. If you have spirits wandering around your house and you can tell them very clearly to get out, they will leave. If you have an illness and you can tell it very clearly to get out, it will leave. You must be honest, however, about what you really want, what you really get out of the condition you have, and what you're really willing to do about it.

## Psychics' Resistance to Being Sick

Sometimes psychics have unique problems in this regard. Because they know all about this stuff, many psychics

141

think it isn't all right for them to be sick. It's like the joke, "If you're so smart, how come you're not rich?" Only this time it goes, "If you're a healer, how come you're sick?" So some healers and other psychics, who don't want to admit to themselves or to other people that they're human just like everybody else, may go around pretending that they never get sick, even when they do. This attitude is a form of resistance, and you know by now what happens when you resist something: You become what you resist. Or, in this case, if you resist being sick, then being sick is probably the next thing on your program.

Amy had a dramatic experience of the effects of resistance when she was just beginning as a healer. A woman came to her with a paralyzed arm. She had had neither an accident nor an illness—she woke up one morning to this dreadful discovery. Amy was sympathetic. She poured attention and energy into this woman, but all to no avail. Other psychics worked on her as well, with the same results.

Finally, Amy gave up, feeling that she had failed her unfortunate client. About half an hour after the healing, she began to notice that her arm was tingling strangely, as it does when an arm or leg falls asleep. Her arm was going numb.

Panicked, Amy told her story to a psychic friend of hers. He patted her on the arm and said, "Well, I guess you'd better go eat an ice cream cone with it." His cure worked.

It was some time before Amy realized that *of course* the woman had not responded to the healings—she didn't want to. She was probably receiving more attention for her paralysis than she ever had for anything in her life, and she wasn't about to give it up to please Amy.

Back in the first chapter of this book we talked a lot about

142

being at one with other people, and with the universe as a whole. You might think that psychics, who have studied this sort of material, and who practice it every day, would have an edge over other mortals in being able to live well without getting caught up in the illusions of life. Unfortunately, this seems to be the case only very rarely. First of all, of course, psychics are people, just like kings, homemakers, tennis players, and children. They are subject to the same fears, desires, and other folderol of being human.

Secondly, *because* they know about this way of working with psychic energy, they sometimes get uppity and think that they have a corner on the living-well market. They think that their lives should be easier than other people's because of the knowledge they possess. In general, this is utter nonsense. The truth of the matter is that the more you know, the greater your responsibilities are. If you know how to type, you can get a job as a stenographer. If you know how to sell, you can get a job as a salesperson. If you know how to manage people and papers, you can get a job as a manager. If you know how to manage managers and run a business, you can get a job as an executive. At every step up the business ladder, your pay gets higher. But at the same time, your responsibilities increase. That's why some people who have PhDs drive taxicabs or work as waitresses: They have decided that they don't want the responsibilities that go along with using their degrees.

In psychic work, as in any other kind of work, the more you know and want to do, the greater your responsibilities become. One of the responsibilities that is an inherent part of psychic work is not to get stuck in ego games. Notice, now, we did not say you couldn't *play* ego games. After all, we all have egos, and what's the good of having an ego if you can't have fun with it? It's there to be played with. What

143

we said was, not to get *stuck* in those games. That is, not to imagine that those games are better or more meaningful than any other games. Not to imagine that just because you can read an aura and cure a headache you won't get head-aches—you will, for sure—or that you're somehow above it all. When a psychic starts thinking that he or she knows more, or is better than, other people, reality will bring him right back down to Earth.

One day while we were writing this book, Bill was feeling pretty cocky. The book was going well, his other work was going well, he had a little money in the bank, he was in love with a wonderful woman who was in love with him—every-thing in his life was working. And he started to think that he really knew his ass from a hole in the ground. He told a couple of his friends about it—not about how well his life was going at that moment, but about how much better it was going to get than it already was. He started outlining his big plans for pie-in-the-sky.

When he left his friends, he got into his car—but sud-denly, and for no apparent reason, it was running badly, coughing and sputtering a lot. He nearly had an accident. At home a friend called and announced that a class in body work he'd been planning to take for several months had been cancelled. A book he was trying to sell for a friend was turned down by the publisher Bill expected to want it. He started to feel like running away to Hawaii and hiding out on a lonely beach. Reality was telling him that he was being a fool.

Admittedly, Bill saw what was going on and the whole episode was over in a couple of hours. Also admittedly, Bill used his psychic knowledge to end the episode, which, a few years ago, might have gone on for days or even weeks.

The point is that just knowing about being psychic does not mean that the sun will always shine on you.

## Healing by Taking on the Disease

In healing, if you forget that you're just another guy or gal, you may find yourself coming down with all the ailments you cure in other people. This is why we taught you about grounding early in the book: If you stay grounded, you are much less likely to get your head in the clouds, since you have your psychic feet planted firmly in the Earth. Still, there are some healers who intentionally work by taking on the illnesses of their clients and then curing themselves of the ailment. As we said earlier, we do not think it is *ever* necessary to do this. Indeed, we strongly advise against it.

If you're a martyr, or a bit masochistic, and you want to find out what it feels like to heal by taking on the disease, experiment on something small, like a headache, instead of something big, like cancer. After you go into your trance, just open your second chakra wide. Then, when you isolate your friend's headache, create it for yourself in your own mind: Where is it located in your head? What color is it? How big is it? What temperature is it? Does it throb or ache? By this time your friend should be feeling fine, and you should be looking for the aspirin. Don't expect any sympathy from your friend for doing this, though. *He* didn't ask you to take on the pain. It's your baby now, and it might be enlightening to ask yourself what you get out of healing with this technique, and whether you want what you're getting.

145

## Working with People Who Have Severe Psychic Disorders

Another problem that sometimes crops up in psychic healing is working with people who are severely disturbed emotionally or psychically. First of all, let us remind you that this book does not train you to be either a physician or a psychiatrist. It is a course in doing psychic healings. If someone comes to you who is really messed up, the kindest, most useful thing you can do for that person is to send him or her to a qualified psychotherapist.

Secondly, you can also—not instead—get down to some basic healing or absent healing. But people with severe psychic or emotional disorders usually have what we call a "hidden agenda." They are getting something very big out of their illness. It may be that they get a whole lot of attention for it; it may be that they relieve themselves of much or all of the responsibility for their own lives by being disturbed; it may be that they have a heavy karmic debt to pay. Whatever it is, they're playing a game with extremely high stakes, and unless you want to play straight-man for them and get suckered into a game that could be painful or even dangerous to you, we advise you to thank them for coming to see you and tell them that you don't do that kind of work. You need not explain yourself or give any reasons. That you say so is reason enough. As we've said before, learning to say "no" can be a very valuable psychic tool.

In one sense, someone who is severely disturbed is probably not willing to be healed in any case. A good psychotherapist may be able to bring such a person to see what his payoff is, and may be able to help him become willing to let go of his games and become well. By doing some absent healing you may be able to help the person's being in this

146

regard, but in all probability that's going to be the limit of what you can do.

## Asking for a Healing You're Not Willing to Have

People who ask for healings and aren't willing to have them are usually playing a game called I Can't and You Can't Make Me. No matter what you do, no matter how good a healer you may be, no matter how great your intention is, you cannot win against such a person's illness. As we've said, you cannot heal a person who isn't willing to be healed. Since psychic healing is about *allowing* another to heal himself rather than *doing* something, when you allow someone to be well who refuses to be well, you haven't accomplished very much. It's like allowing the rain to fall on an absolutely cloudless day. You'd be better off allowing the sun to shine.

It will make your work easier to ask the person who comes to you for a healing if he or she is willing to be healed, and then, when you go into trance to do your reading, take a close look at this question again, and ask the person's being if *it* is willing to have the healing. As we pointed out earlier, you may often find that the person is not letting you in, and bringing the issue out in front, talking about it, usually clears it up. Most of the time someone who isn't willing to be healed doesn't even know that's his position. If you can point it out to him by asking about it, he may be able to bring his feelings up to a conscious level and gain the power of choice over them. Then he can choose to be healed or not, and you can work accordingly.

## Drugs

Sometimes a person won't be willing to be healed if he or she feels he'll have to give up something in exchange or as a result of the healing. For instance, people who have been taking drugs for a long time may have built up a kind of dependency—physical or psychological—on their favorite drug or drugs. If someone's been taking Valium every day for six years, his mind is likely to have some survival attached to popping that pill each morning. If you say, "Throw away your Valium and walk!" his mind may not be able to handle it.

People who take a lot of drugs usually—not always—need a lot of survival assurance if you're going to heal them successfully. Their minds need to know that they won't die if they're healed, or if they give up their pills. Sometimes people who use drugs are not willing to acknowledge this part of their behavior. Yet, if you're to work with them successfully, it is useful to know what you're up against.

The first step in finding out if a person is using drugs is to ask, and then if the answer doesn't satisfy you, take a look psychically. When healing a person who uses drugs, assure his or her being that it can have the drug if it wants it, and that it can also give up the drug if it wants to do that. Beings are often willing to give up drugs that minds and bodies want to keep.

In healing a person who uses drugs, ground him well through his first chakra and also through his feet. Clean out his first chakra thoroughly, and fill it with gold or blue energy, depending on whether he needs to be soothed (blue) or enlivened (gold). And when the healing is over, have him do something to make his body real without the drug.

148

We are not saying drugs are bad. Drugs are drugs. The use to which a drug is put may be seen as good, bad, or indifferent. We are simply noting for you that people who have become habituated to some drug or drugs are liable to go "into survival" easily, especially if they feel their drugs may be taken away from them. By drugs we mean not only tranquilizers and energizers but also marijuana, alcohol, tobacco, and coffee.

## Death and Dying

We've talked about survival periodically in this book and discussed how people are likely to go "into survival" when they feel severely threatened. Survival is that which is opposite to death. And death itself is, for most people, the Great Unknown. In a manner of speaking, it is the big—the really big—change.

Earlier in this book we mentioned Bill's friend who was killed by an automobile and who then began to "haunt" his apartment. It seems that some spirits are reluctant to leave the physical plane after their bodies die, either because they liked it here, or because they have some unfinished business among the living, or because they are momentarily confused about which plane of existence they belong on.

Recent studies suggest that death is neither the Heaven/- Hell concept some churches teach, nor the Big Nothing the so-called rational philosophers would have us believe. Medical doctors such as Elisabeth Kübler-Ross and Raymond S. Moody have spent many hours with people as they died, and with other people who died medically but were brought back to life. And these people tell some extraordinary tales of what it was like for them to die and to be dead. Their experiences coincide with the experiences psychics and mystics have described for thousands of years.

In Dr. Moody's book, *Life After Life,* he constructs a "theoretically 'ideal' or 'complete' experience which embodies all of the common elements" that he found present in the vast majority of the more than 150 cases of death-and-resuscitation which he studied. It is pertinent to this book:

> A man is dying and, as he reaches the point of greater physical distress, he hears himself pronounced dead by his doctor. He begins to hear an uncomfortable noise, a loud ringing or buzzing, and at the same time feels himself moving very rapidly through a long dark tunnel. After this, he suddenly finds himself outside of his own physical body, but still in the immediate physical environment, and he sees his own body from a distance, as though he is a spectator. He watches the resuscitation attempt from this unusual vantage point and is in a state of emotional upheaval.
>
> After a while, he collects himself and becomes more accustomed to his odd condition. He notices that he still has a "body," but one of a very different nature and with very different powers from the physical body he has left behind. Soon other things begin to happen. Others come to meet and help him. He glimpses the spirits of relatives and friends who have already died, and a loving warm spirit of a kind he has never encountered before—a being of light—appears before him. This being asks him a question, nonverbally, to make him evaluate his life and helps him along by showing him a panoramic, instantaneous playback of the major events of his life. At some point he finds himself approaching some sort of barrier or border, apparently representing the limit between earthly life and the next life. Yet, he finds that he must go back to the earth, that the time for his death

has not yet come. At this point he resists, for by now he is taken up with his experiences in the afterlife and does not want to return. He is overwhelmed by intense feelings of joy, love, and peace. Despite his attitude, though, he somehow reunites with his physical body and lives.*

*Raymond A. Moody, M.D., *Life After Life* (New York: Bantam Books, 1975, pp. 21–22).

The people with whom Dr. Moody worked were among the very few of us on Earth who could say with certainty what death was, for them. The rest of us can rely on those people's personal experiences, or on the belief systems we have been trained all our lives to accept (see Chapter 7)— including the belief system that says we cannot know about death.

Neither Amy nor Bill has had the experience of dying in this lifetime. Yet our experiences with others' deaths, and our experiences as healers, suggest to us that death is, among other things, a great teacher of the soul, defining and clarifying the experiences of a lifetime rather in the way illness defines and clarifies the experience of being well.

Because it is such a major event in a person's life, and because it is so entirely unknown—in most living people's personal experience—death is ordinarily feared above all else. When life situations become particularly stressful, or otherwise frightening, the body's great fear is that it will cease to exist. *All* fear responses, then, are determined to some extent by a person's fear of his own death. When you are frightened by a spider, or by a nightmare, or by some strange shadow lurking in your doorway late at night, you are, at some level, in fear of dying.

In any state of fear the body goes into survival as its psychic reaction. In fear, the body reacts out of the first chakra, releasing its stores of survival knowledge in order to maintain its life.

Most fear situations do not really demand such an extreme response. Very, very few spiders are deadly. Most nightmares do not pertain to death but rather to the problems of living. And most lurking shadows turn out to be trees, cats, or neighbors searching for lost house keys.

Most of the situations that generate survival fears would, more appropriately, generate responses from the various nonsurvival energy centers—emotions, communication, intuition, etc. The body, however, may be expected not to know this, and will utilize all fear to send out the most dire danger signals it can awaken in you.

Every time you "give in" to the fear that provokes such extreme responses, you necessarily deepen the power such fear has over your life. And every time you accept such fear simply for what it is—a powerful reaction to a usually mild stimulus—you decrease its potency. Perhaps this is why people who have already experienced their own deaths—such as those studied by Dr. Moody—and many people who have been literally at the edge of death—such as survivors of the Nazi concentration camps, or the survivors of accidents and other cataclysmic disasters such as earthquakes —seem to be calm and graceful under the stresses that send the rest of us into intense survival patterns. Survival patterns may be obvious, as when, seeing a strange person skulking in our doorway late at night, the adrenaline rushes through our systems, preparing us for fight or flight. But they may also be less obvious, as when, confronted by a situation we feel as if we "can't face," we become extremely lethargic, tired, or bored. Wanting to go to sleep, like wanting to run away physically, is often a psychic avoidance pattern, designed to save us from having to reckon with that which we fear. A stressful encounter which is obviously not fatally dangerous is liable to set off more sophisticated, covert fear responses than a rush of adrenaline since it is too patently obvious that a clear "fear" response—fight or flight—is not appropriate. These people have learned something through their experiences with death that the rest of us have spent enormous quantities of energy avoiding. And out of their confrontations with death, they have earned a certain amount of serenity in the face of all fears.

Certainly such people still become frightened. But their fears seem to possess a quality unlike those the rest of us experience when we have not learned that we will not die from what we fear, and when we have not learned that our death itself is not necessarily the end of the line for our conscious beings.

As a healer you will have the opportunity to witness many versions of fear. People who ask you to heal them will usually be in fear—either fear that you will be successful, which their minds may not be able to comprehend, or that they will have to give up their illness; or fear that you'll fail and leave them with their ailments. When you do readings associated with healings, you will see a great deal of unconfronted fear and numerous fear symbols in people's auras. Sometimes you will be able to help them to see their fears, and sometimes not. Usually, however, if you see fear in a person's energy body, you will find it relates to his illness in a surprisingly simple and direct way.

Whenever you read fear in a person's energy body, pay particular attention to his first chakra, his feet chakras, and his grounding cord. When these are clean and firm, his body will be assured of its safety, and the person will free up large amounts of psychic energy with which to work on other energy centers and other problems.

As a healer you will also see a lot of your own fear. No matter how much the material in this book, and in your own experience, becomes clear to you, and no matter how much work you do in psychic realms, you are still living in the physical, material world. You still have a body, you are still alive, and you will someday have to confront your own death.

Because death will remain a mysterious experience to you until you die, and because your primary focus in this lifetime is a material one, your fear of death—and therefore of other, lesser life problems—will probably always be with you. In all probability your death is not an issue you will resolve until you die. Since your death will be—is—a constant companion, always wearing your clothes, always sleeping beside you, and present in your every word and deed, you might as well get on good terms with it. When you resist your fear of death, you will always be frightened of dying. And this fear will enter into every aspect of your life. On the other hand, when you acknowledge your death and your fear of it, you open a psychic space in your life for you and your death to get along, for you to see your own death as a part of your life. And then the fear can begin to dissipate and free you—as it frees your friends when you work with them—to be more fully in touch with your life.

Back in Chapter 1, when we talked about colors, we spoke of the color black as "the color of death and destruction." We also said, however, that "death is the state that precedes rebirth, and destruction is the state that precedes construction, or creativity." As black can be seen as an extremely positive color, so death, for all our fears of it, can be seen as an extremely positive happening—the life-event which fulfills us completely and finally, and frees us for the next great adventure. When we speak of death as a teacher, it is this that we mean: confronting and acknowledging the fear, and coming to own it, so that we may be freer.

The question "Why do people get sick?" might be altered to read, "Why do people die?" And really, who knows why people die? But it seems that those who choose to do so appear to learn something of their soul's purposes through coming to terms with the experience of death.

In the largest and, perhaps, most psychic senses, people seem to get sick as a way of learning something about their journeys through the physical plane. They learn to meet their fears and wishes, they learn about their relationships to life and to their bodies, and they learn something about who they truly are—not who their bodies are, or who their minds are, or who their intellects are, or who their emotions are, although they learn that too, and learn that each of these things is a part of them. But who *they* are—who the being, or soul, or entity is that lies beneath the trappings of material existence, and who has clothed itself in material forms for the purpose of being here on Earth, in physical form, to learn, to love, and to grow.

## The Karmic Connections

There is information here about karma, too. In Buddhist mythology there is a kind of person know as a bodhisattva (bow-dee-SAHT-vah). A bodhisattva is someone who is destined to be a Buddha (a totally awakened, or enlightened, being), but who has pledged that instead of living in the state of enlightenment alone, he will return to mortal, physical form again and again, for the purpose of helping all sentient beings to become enlightened. Buddhists feel

155

that Gautama Buddha himself, like Jesus Christ, was such a being. And indeed, if we look at the teachings of these and other great healers, psychics, and messengers of God, we find that they saw so clearly that we are all one that it would be impossible for them to sit smiling in some benign heaven or nirvana waiting for the rest of us to catch up. Because they saw that we and they are the same, and that, finally, there is no enlightenment for one person which does not entail enlightenment for all, and that as long as one person lives in psychic darkness, we all share his burden.

Thus it would seem that we all must live and die and live and die and live again, until living and dying become, for each of us, simply different faces of the single process in which we recognize that, as gods indeed, we are each and all a part of everything. And that our lives and our deaths each participate in the great process of becoming, as we simply come to see the face of God without fear, and come to be a part of it.

# 7

# FAITH,
# BELIEF SYSTEMS,
# AND DREAMS

## Faith, Belief, Intuition, and Surrender

*Faith* is belief which is not based on proof. *Belief* is a
conviction of truth or reality without positive knowledge.

In Chapter 1 we told you that if what we say in this book
is not true for you in your own experience, then it is, in the
realest sense, not true. It is important that you not *believe*
what we say here, and it is important that you not have *faith*
in any of this material. We cannot provide proof or positive
knowledge for you that anything we say is so. Unless you
have some experience of your own that validates our
claims, then you have nothing to go on but our opinions,
which may be totally meaningless in the context of your
own life. You don't even know us. We may be totally mad.

One purpose of the exercises we suggest in this book is

157

to teach you the nuts and bolts of the process of psychic healing. Another purpose—and in the long run, the more valuable one—is to guide you to direct, personal experiences of your own psychic abilities. These experiences, whatever they are, will be your proof. They will carry you past belief to positive knowledge.

Ultimately, you see, there is no way to learn this stuff except through knowing it, which is the seventh chakra function of pure intuition. Intuition differs from belief in part because it has no system. Intuition is always a process, and it is always new. In a system of belief, certain things are always assumed. Intuition assumes nothing: It knows.

Faith is sometimes powerful and sometimes weak. But where faith is a relief, intuition is a release; where faith is comfort, intuition is surrender. Faith, like belief, is founded on expectations: If I do *abc,* then *xyz* will result. Any system is based on expectations, and any expectation contains the seed of disappointment. If you think you're going to get something by loving someone, the thing you're most likely to get is disappointment.

Surrender is not a system. It implies no expectations and, therefore, no disappointments. If you love someone just because you love, then you surrender to love, you give it away instead of trading it. And how much love you have when you give it away!

Surrender is not a matter of submitting to a competing force. Surrender is being in neutral. It is nonresistance. It is having things the way they are.

In one sense, this is a book about surrender and giving away your power. Only in giving away your power do you come to surrender, and the only thing you can surrender to is what is. When you surrender to what is, you are totally nonresistant, totally neutral, totally intuitive; and, ironi-

158

cally, you become totally powerful. You become an inherent and essential part of what is. Actually, you don't *become* what already is, since you already *are*. It is more accurate to say that you *recognize* that you are a part of what is. It is valuable to *experience* the truth of this condition, because it is so much more apparent at an intellectual level that we often fail to grasp the astonishing power behind this simple fact.

We said at the end of Chapter 4 that the process of psychic reading is actually the process of talking to yourself, about yourself. In the same way, any psychic process is a matter of surrendering to yourself.

Surrender, neutrality, nonresistance—all these are handles for latching onto the harmony of the universe. To the degree you are at one with this harmony, you are psychic. But if you *believe* in the harmony of the cosmos, or if you have *faith* in it, then you expect it to behave in a particular, preconditioned way. As a result, you are off balance, resistant, and out of harmony.

## Belief Systems

A belief system is a structure of assumptions on the basis of which we pretend to know how things work. When I turn on my lamp, I believe the light is going to go on. I have faith in the system of electricity which begins, for all practical purposes, with some large body of water I've never seen being channeled through machines it confuses me to even think about. Somehow, these machines create or extract a force which is sent out through hundreds or thousands of miles of copper wire. The force reaches my house and waits

159

inside my walls like an obedient servant until I call it forth with a flick of a switch.

I pretend that I know how electricity works, because when I flick that switch my lamp goes on. But when I flick the switch and my lamp *doesn't* go on—because a power line is down, or because a fuse blew out, or even because my light bulb is burned out—my expectations are disappointed and I get a little upset. I am confronted with the fact that, for me, electricity is nothing more or less than magic.

In psychic work, we have the opportunity to confront a lot of assumptions and a lot of belief systems, both our own and those of the people we read or heal. And the farther back we go into most people's situations, the more we see that their whole lives are based on one form of magic or another. This is because, for most people, there will always be some questions to which there is only one true answer: I don't know.

Sometimes it's easy to acknowledge that you don't know. For instance, if you ask me how electricity works, I'll be glad to tell you that I don't know. But sometimes the questions are harder and trickier, and the answers we think we have turn out to beget even more impossible questions. For example, Why are there people on Earth? Whatever your answer is, I will ask you how you know your answer is correct. Eventually, we will arrive at the answer to all the questions about your answers, and we will have arrived at one of your fundamental assumptions. In other words, we will have arrived at one of the building blocks of your personal belief system.

Your belief system creates your personal reality. If you believe that the world is an evil place, you will experience evil in the world, and the evil you experience will justify your belief that the world is an evil place. By the same token, if you believe the world is a benevolent place, you will experience benevolence, and the benevolence you experience will justify your belief that the world is a benevolent place.

In Chapter 4, when we spoke about "havingness," we implied something about belief. If your financial havingness level extends, say, to $100, then it is demonstrable that you believe you can have $100, because you *do* have $100.

A friend of Bill's, who is a real estate broker, found that several salespeople he employed had very specific havingness levels. One man, working on commission, earned between $47,000 and $53,000 year in and year out for the six or seven years he worked for Bill's friend. Another man, also working on commission, earned *almost* $15,000 every year but could never break through that particular number. The first man had a consistent havingness level of about $50,000—that was the amount of money he could have through earnings in a year. The second man did not believe he could earn $15,000. Both men worked through good and bad years in the real estate market, yet their earnings were quite different from each other's while remaining about the same for themselves, year after year.

Belief systems affect all facets of your life, including your health and well-being. If you believe that eating dog food will keep you healthy, you'd better eat dog food. If you believe that eating fatty foods will give you pimples, indeed it will. If you believe you're destined to be blind, the chances are excellent that you'll become blind.

There are two principal difficulties arising from belief systems. The first is that if your personal reality clashes with the world's reality, you are likely to suffer guilt about your own behavior, and resentment toward others about theirs. The second difficulty is that belief systems are limiting. If you believe you will be blind, for instance, you are not free to be anything *but* blind.

It is important to isolate and define your beliefs so that you can own them instead of being owned by them. To own a belief is to escape its inevitability and to become free to choose whether or not you want the belief and its implications.

The good thing about belief systems is that they can be changed. Since a belief system is only one way of seeing or understanding, any other way of seeing or understanding can be substituted for it. No single system is more "right" than any other system.

The interpretation, or system, that is most right for a person at any given moment is the one that works best for him at that moment—the one that provides him with maximum satisfaction. If you are feeling ill, probably something is out of joint in your relationship with the cosmos. If you examine yourself psychically, you will be able to ascertain what is out, and what to do to put it back in. The same holds true for examining others psychically.

This book is, to a large extent, predicated on a kind of system. It is not so much a system that we believe in, as it is one which has worked for us, and which we have observed works for others. Yet, there will be some value in our pointing out to you that we *are* teaching you a system. And if we are successful, you will eventually discard this system along with any others you may have stashed away in your head.

There is an ancient paradox which, translated into a contemporary bumper sticker, reads: *This statement is false.* The paradox, of course, is that if the statement is false, then it is true; whereas, if the statement is true, then it is false.

In a sense, that sort of paradox applies to this book. By now we may have given you the impression that you have to "do" something in order to effect a healing. Not so. You don't have to clean chakras or run energy or diddle around with auras. You don't have to pull cords or keep out of anyone's psychic space or mock up roses. You don't have to talk to your body or look at colors or even pay attention.

All you have to do to effect a healing is to let your friend have his symptoms, his ailments, his complaints, and intend that he be well. If your friend doesn't feel well, let him not feel well. Since he doesn't feel well already, letting him feel the way he feels should be pretty easy.

But it isn't. Letting things be the way they are is extremely hard. Everyone has a picture of how things "should" be, or how things will be when they are "right," or how the person who feels ill will feel when he's "well." As you become what you resist, so other people, the world, and the cosmos also become what you resist their becoming. When you do not resist the way things are, those things have the psychic space to finish being the way they are, and to move on to being whatever they are next. To effect a healing, then, you surrender.

## Faith Healing

It is a curious thing for us to say, but the less a healer *cares* about the results of his healing, the more potent a healer he can be. This is because the most powerful healings are effected from a state of true love—fourth chakra affinity—in which the heart is loving for love's sake alone.

When you love someone so that he or she will give you

163

security, or money, or attention, you are not loving for the sheer joy of loving. You are loving to acquire something in return. Perhaps, between two specific people, a satisfying agreement can exist: "I will give you love if you will give me money (security, attention, etc.)." But more often, confusion results. Many things are demanded in the name of love, including money, security, attention, promises, conditions, and so on. And often love itself is lost because it did not find fulfillment in itself.

It is the same with healing. When a healer heals because he loves to heal, the healing has the greatest possibility of taking place. When a healer heals because he wants to have his ego stroked for being a Good Healer, or because he doesn't want someone he loves to die or be ill (and, by extension, to leave him), or because he wants to be a Famous Healer and have everyone hear about his successes, then his mind is elsewhere as he heals. His wishes siphon off his energy. The healing energy must go to support his wishes instead of to healing. But if he can, for a moment, put aside his personal desires, he can become an absolutely clear channel for the healing energies.

Every time Amy heals, she experiences the exquisite pleasure of being a channel for bright, cleansing energy. Her own physical and psychic bodies are healed as she heals others. She experiences states of delight, peace, power, tranquility—all from feeling the many energies.

Many healers say, "God works through me—I don't know what I do." It is not necessary to know what you do. As we've said, ultimately you do not need to clean auras, pull cords, make roses, and so on. You need only intend for the healing to take place. When a healer claims to be a channel for God, it is his or her own personal God— whether that is a God in heaven or the God of his or her own heart.

164

The "faith" of a faith healer is not so much faith, perhaps, as it is that pure condition of fourth chakra love that requires nothing in return. And the miraculous cures sometimes effected by such healers take place in a condition of surrender.

A faith healer has no energy in his client's illness or health. He has no *need* for the person to feel better, and has none of his own survival pictures locked up in whether or not someone recovers. The healer can operate from an intention which utilizes the harmonious, neutral energy of the cosmos instead of his own energy.

In his condition of neutrality, the faith healer can give his client the psychic space to be ill: he does not have to resist the person's ailments. Then, when the healer is not resisting the illness, the person who is ill is not resisting the illness, and the illness is not resisting either of them, the faith healer can choose—from his heart, and without striving—for the illness to disappear.

As a healer, when you want a result, you are planning. If you are planning, you are not in the here and now giving a healing: You are five minutes in the future, or an hour or a lifetime in the future, enjoying the imagined results of your work.

Faith healing has a reputation for being almost corny, conjuring up images of fanatic worshippers shouting, chanting, and beating their breasts in a kind of pagan ritual prayer to God. While that image may be unattractive to many people, the process that makes a revival-hall healing work is the same one that makes an aura cleaning work. In a revival-hall situation, the healing is facilitated by a strong *group* intention rather than just the intention of one healer. When this kind of faith is completely secure, it does not question with its mind—it succeeds through pure will.

The process by which a healer "lays hands" on someone

and effects a healing is exactly like the healing processes we've been teaching you in this book, except that direct, physical contact takes place. Healers who work by laying on hands, like psychic surgeons, find that the direct touch helps them to focus their attention and energies to the ailing part of the body.

We have found that touching often makes a person feel more secure about having a healing. In a sense, touch helps make a person's body "real." Yet, we have not found it necessary to use physical contact in most healings. Of course, under the best of circumstances you should avoid laying your hands on certain people, or on certain parts of the anatomy of any person who comes to you for a healing. Be appropriate to the situation, and don't do things that will obstruct the result you're after—which is effecting cures psychically.

Émile Coué was a French psychologist at the turn of the last century, who advocated autosuggestion. It was Coué's contention that if a person told himself that something was true for a long enough period of time, that thing would become true. "Every day in every way I am getting better and better" were his exact words.

In a way, the exercises Coué offered were a kind of self-hypnosis designed to change a person's belief systems. Except that they were directed toward helping people, instead of selling goods, Coué's ideas were not much different than those of the advertising moguls of Madison Avenue. How many products do you use simply because you've heard often enough, or loudly enough, or from a sufficiently authoritative source that they're good, or good for you, or something like that? These are products which you may not need, and which, when you come right down to it, you may not even *want*. Yet you use them because you believe in them.

Belief, obviously, does not begin in the conscious mind, but rather in that part of us that accepts "a conviction of truth or reality without positive knowledge."

Here are two simple exercises for getting in touch with some of your own belief systems. The exercises stretch over many days, although they only require a few minutes' attention on any one day. Since you've been observing yourself and paying attention for several chapters now, the exercises should be very easy and should provide you with a lot of information about your beliefs.

## Belief Exercise #1

1. Select any *one* thing that you do habitually. It may be something you like, something you dislike, or something you don't care about, but start with only one item so that you can devote your attention to it for this exercise.

2. Every time you do this thing for the next two weeks, don't do anything else at the same time. If your item is the way you say goodnight to your spouse, don't kiss him or her at the same time you say goodnight; don't say goodnight while brushing your teeth; don't say goodnight from behind your book or newspaper. Just pay complete attention to saying goodnight. If your item is smoking cigarettes, don't smoke and drink coffee at the same time; don't smoke and talk at the same time; don't smoke and read at the same time. Just smoke.

3. During the two-week test period, notice what your mind says to you about this exercise. Notice if it tells you

that this exercise is silly; notice if it wanders so that you forget to do the exercise; notice if it keeps you in your rut; notice if it takes on a *new* automatic way of handling this habit. If you habitually say goodnight to your spouse while brushing your teeth, notice if this habit brings you closer to him or her, or keeps you at a distance, or something else. If you habitually smoke a cigarette with your coffee, notice if this habit brings you the satisfaction you expect from your coffee and/or your cigarette.

4. During the two-week test period, notice what the payoff is for your habit, and notice where your habit began. When you find out where your habit began, see what belief motivated it. If you say goodnight to your spouse while brushing your teeth, do you believe you're saving time? If you smoke a cigarette with your coffee, do you believe the two things make an "adult" combination? And so on.

5. At the end of the two-week test period, go back to your old way of doing your item for one day. Notice if it feels any different than it used to. On the second day after the test period, choose which way you want to do your item. Do it any way you like, but know that you are choosing that way, and don't do it out of a belief system.

## Belief Exercise #2

1. Select any *one* thing that you do not like about yourself. You can use anything, but it will be easier to do this exercise if you choose something obvious, such as being too fat or too thin or too poor.

2. Every morning when you get up, and every evening when you are getting ready to go to bed, and at least once

a day in between, say to yourself in the mirror, "I (your name) give myself permission to (be thin, be heavy, have money, etc.)."

3. Do this exercise until the person in the mirror responds to you. We can't tell you what this will look like, or how long it will take, but you'll know it when you see it.

4. As you do this exercise, see what you believe about the condition you want to change. Do you believe that fat (or thin) people get more (or less) love? Do you believe you *can* have money? Etc.


## Success and Failure

It is sometimes puzzling that one person is wildly successful in business, or love, or athletics, while another person—clearly as gifted and hard-working as the first—totters on the edge of failure all his life. It is also puzzling that some of the most successful people are dissatisfied with their lots and find that success is not the fountain of satisfaction and well-being they had thought it would be, while some people who never seem to get much in the way of material reward are rich in the pleasures of life.

To be sure, success and dissatisfaction, or failure and satisfaction, do not go hand in hand by any means; and most people we have met would rather be successful *and* satisfied than any other combination of possibilities. But people who are successful and satisfied, or unsuccessful and unsatisfied, don't cause us many questions—those seem like "normal" states. It is, as usual, the exception that makes us notice what the rule is.

In the day-to-day world, success and failure seem like

169

polar opposites, and in our goal-oriented, technological society, they are usually *treated* as opposites. Yet, as illness is a facet of health, so failure is a facet of success. And as it is not really possible to be ill, so it is not really possible to fail.

Perhaps these preceding comments require a little explanation. We said in Chapter 5 that healing is not so much the process of correcting that which isn't working as it is the process of allowing things to be the way they are. We have also talked, recently, about the harmony and flow of the cosmos. *It is not possible to be out of this flow, and it is not possible to prevent the process of things working.* By the same token, it is not possible to be "ill." However, it is very possible not to *recognize* the flow, or to *think* that things are not working, or to *feel* unwell.

In addition to its value as mental aspirin, psychic healing is a process of restoring the awareness that everything in the universe is unfolding exactly as it is supposed to, and restoring the awareness that each individual is the creator of his or her experience. When we work with chakras, auras, and energy bodies, we are working with a kind of language for dealing with these forces and for allowing ourselves back into the harmonious flow. We are in that flow, even when it doesn't look that way to us.

One approach to grasping this rather flighty and nebulous concept is to grasp the relationship between success and failure, and then to apply it as an equivalent relationship between health and illness. We are working here toward the recognition that illness is a part of health, as failure is a part of success.

1. Go into trance.

2. Mock up your picture of being successful, whatever that is, on your mental screen.

170

3. On a separate but equal screen, mock up your picture of failure.

4. Pretend that success is more important than failure.

5. Pretend that failure is more important than success.

6. Repeat steps 4 and 5 several times.

7. Place your picture of success over your picture of failure.

8. Place your picture of failure over your picture of success.

9. Repeat steps 7 and 8 several times.

10. Come out of trance.

As you did the preceding exercise, did the distinctions between your picture of "success" and your picture of "failure" begin to blur?

1. Go into trance.

2. Mock up your picture of being healthy on your mental screen.

3. On a separate but equal screen, mock up your picture of illness.

4. Pretend that health is better than illness.

5. Pretend that illness is better than health.

6. Repeat steps 4 and 5 several times.

7. Place your picture of health over your picture of illness.

8. Place your picture of illness over your picture of health.

9. Repeat steps 7 and 8 several times.

10. Come out of trance.

Success and failure are intimately associated with health and illness. Since everything is unfolding exactly as it is supposed to, when you fail, you are succeeding at failing. Once again, watch for the payoff. If you fail habitually, what do you get out of it? Do you get sympathy? Attention? Do you get to feel bad, or to irritate your father, mother, etc.? Many people who fail a lot find that the big payoff is that they don't have to take responsibility for being good enough to succeed, and for showing their power to themselves and the world. When you feel unwell, your body is calling attention to the fact that you are not recognizing the flow, and it is providing you with an opportunity to get back in touch with your natural self.

### Creating and Destroying

Just as we tend to believe that success is different from failure, and health is different from illness, so we also tend to think that creating is different from destroying. When we do not recognize the larger context in which all these apparent dichotomies exist, we get stuck in our pictures of the differences between them, and as a result, we resist the parts which we regard as negative.

The following exercise is designed to put you in touch with your abilities to create and destroy.

1. Go into trance.

2. Create an illness. It can be a small illness, like a headache, or it can be a large illness, like leprosy. Be imaginative, have fun—this is a game.

3. Destroy the illness you have created.

4. Mock up another illness and destroy it.

5. Create a third illness.

6. Leaving this third illness alone, create two more illnesses.

7. Destroy all the illnesses you have created.

8. Mock up three new illnesses.

172

9. Mock up twice as many illnesses as you have mocked up altogether so far.

10. Now destroy all the illnesses you have created so far.

11. Destroy three more illnesses than you have created so far.

12. Create a brand-new illness.

13. Create a hundred brand-new illnesses.

14. Create as many brand-new illnesses as there are microbes in the universe.

15. Destroy twice as many illnesses as there are microbes in the universe.

16. Create and destroy as many illnesses as you wish.

17. Dissolve all your pictures and come out of trance.

We are the creators of our experiences. We create our health and we create our illnesses, just as we create our successes and failures.

## Scarcity

Part of the problem people seem to have in being successful or in creating the health they want is that most of us believe in scarcity. We believe there isn't enough success, health, money, love, or whatever to go around. And since, in addition, most of us don't believe we *deserve* to have anything we want, including perfect health, we limit the success, health, etc., that we allow ourselves to have.

When things are scarce in your life, it's generally because you believe there isn't enough to go around or to satisfy you. As a result you hoard what little you have. And as a result of hoarding, you make scarcity—once a belief—into a reality for yourself.

173

Let's take the example of love. If you have a little love in your life, and you hold onto it for fear you'll never have any more, you become tight, self-protective, and bent over—spiritually if not physically. But if you have a little love in your life and you give it away, you find immediately that you have even more love in your life. In fact, the more love you give away, the more love you have.

Now, if you give your love away *in order to get more,* you're not giving it away at all—you are coming from a condition of scarcity rather than from a condition of sufficiency, because you think you want, need, or should have more love than you have to begin with. If you give love away from such a condition, it is not love you're putting out into the world, but need. And what you'll get back is more need.

When the Bible advises, "Cast your bread upon the waters and it shall return threefold," it is not kidding. But you must give it away simply to give it away, or you're really doing something else altogether. And it is the something else—the thing you're really doing, the thing that underlies your pretense—that will come back to you.

It is not possible to lie to the cosmic harmony; it is only possible to tell the truth. When you do anything other than tell the truth, you fool yourself. And you will learn that you fooled yourself when you see what comes back to you. "As you sow," the Book says, "so shall you reap." Not as you *think* or *believe* you sow.

The following two-part exercise may seem a little complicated. Read it over a couple of times before you do it to make sure you understand the instructions.

1. Go into trance.

2. Create some scarcity—that is, create in your mind a condition of *not enough,* or *need.*

3. Create some more scarcity. Create so much scarcity that the universe is taken over by scarcity.

4. When scarcity is extremely plentiful, and there just isn't enough of *anything,* ask yourself if that's *enough scarcity.* If it is not enough scarcity, create twice as much scarcity as you've created so far. Keep doubling the amount of scarcity you have in the universe until there's enough of it.

5. When you have enough scarcity, leave that universe alone and create a whole new universe that has *no scarcity at all.*

6. In this second universe, create some sufficiency—that is, create a condition of *enough.* When there's plenty of sufficiency, ask yourself if there's *enough sufficiency.* If not, create some more. Create sufficiency until there's a sufficiency of sufficiency—enough of it—in your second universe.

7. Put your two universes side by side on your mental screen, leaving some space around them and between them.

8. Fill the empty space with scarcity from your first universe. Fill the space completely.

9. Now, is your first universe missing any scarcity? If so, create some more and fill it back up.

10. Fill the space with sufficiency from your second universe. Again, fill the space completely.

11. Is your second universe missing any sufficiency? If so, create some more and fill it back up.

12. Repeat steps 8–11 until you know who it is who creates scarcity and sufficiency in your universe.

13. Dissolve all your pictures and come out of trance.

Open your eyes and take a look around the room. Does it appear any different to you than it did before this exercise?

1. Go back into trance.

2. On your mental screen, mock up a picture of yourself.

3. Ask yourself if you have a scarcity of anything—love,

money, health, anything. If the answer is "no," go on to step 4. If the answer is "yes," ask yourself what you have a scarcity of. Go to your universe of sufficiency and take some of whatever it is you need and bring it back and give it to the picture of yourself. Do this until you have enough of whatever it is you need.

4. When you have enough, make a picture of someone else on a separate screen, and give that person some of whatever you just gave yourself.

5. Ask yourself if you still have enough of what you just gave away. If you have, go on to step 6. If you have not, go to your universe of sufficiency and get some more for yourself. Then give some away again. Repeat this step until you can give it away and still have enough.

6. If your universe of sufficiency has been depleted by this exercise, fill it up with more sufficiency.

7. Dissolve all your pictures and come out of trance.

Did you find that as you gave it away your own pile grew, diminished, or stayed the same? Is that what you'd like it to do in the future? If not, do the exercise again, and postulate that every time you give it away, your own pile grows bigger, or smaller, or stays the same—whatever you want it to do.

## Dreams, Dream Healing, and Astral Classes

Who knows where dreams come from, or where they go, or what their ultimate use or purpose may be? From ancient times it has been thought that dreams reveal the Divine Will to man. In Norse mythology dreams were thought to be the medium through which the dead communicated with the living. A tribe of Australian bushmen has a saying that "There is a dream dreaming us."

Seers, prophets, poets, and psychoanalysts have all had a hand in delineating the importance of dream symbology. Over the past couple of decades several researchers working in sleep laboratories have drawn positive correlations between dreams, ESP, and precognition. The Yaqui Indian sorcerer, don Juan, taught Carlos Castaneda to use his dreams as a way of becoming a man of knowledge.

We have said from time to time that you are the creator of your own experience. Nowhere is this truth so clear as in the province of dreams, for here there is no apparency of an external reality to confuse you. Even if God or the dead do communicate with you in your dreams, the landscape, characters, plot, narration, and symbology all exist as constructs of your imagination, reflecting and reflected in the visual language of your mind.

Our experience with dreams suggests that they fulfill many functions, all of which fall within the larger context of the being and mind communicating with each other. Since the being is aware of its connection with the cosmic harmony, it can feed information to the mind in ways the mind can understand and use to further its own psychic growth. In the same way, dreams can be used in all areas of psychic work, including healing.

While we were writing the early chapters of this book, a close friend of Bill's found out that she had uterine cancer. Although she was about to start radiation therapy leading to surgery, Bill asked her if she would like to receive an absent healing. She laughed and said, "If not now, when?"

About a week later, Bill and Amy sat down together one afternoon and performed an absent healing for Bill's friend, very similar to the exercise you learned in Chapter

177

2. A couple of days later, Bill spoke with her by telephone. She said, "I had the strangest dream the other night. I dreamed you took me to a large house full of people I had never seen before. I remember a lot of golden light."

Bill asked if she remembered any of the people in the house. She said, "You know, it's funny, but I can only remember one of the people clearly," and she proceeded to describe a woman who could only have been Amy, although she and Amy had never met, and she had no idea what Amy looked like. At her next medical examination, the cancer had stopped growing. She continued with standard medical treatment and the cancer-free uterus was removed surgically a couple of months after this incident. Allopathic physicians may say that the radiation therapy cured the cancer; psychics may say that the absent healing cured the cancer. We suggest that Bill's friend cured the cancer, creating in her universe powerful assistance from both sources.

We have found the dream world an ideal place to do psychic work. In the dream state you are already focused in a reality other than your usual one, and much dream work can be accomplished simply by setting your mind to the task before falling asleep. The first step in doing any dream work is to establish contact with your own dream world. It has been demonstrated through various scientific experiments that everyone dreams at night, during specific stages of sleep. So you don't have to wait for a night on which you have dreams; the issue is not whether you have them, but whether you recall them.

The most effective way to recall your dreams is to wake yourself up when you have a dream. You can encourage yourself to believe you mean it by setting a pad of paper and a pen beside your bed at night. Then, as you get into bed, go into a light trance just as if you were going to do a reading or a healing. You can go into this trance lying down if you wish. Once you're in trance and grounded, communicate to yourself very clearly that you want to awaken with your dreams. Then drift off to sleep.

Some people find that they can wake up with their dreams the first night they do this exercise. Others require a few days. When Bill started doing dream work, he began by dreaming that he woke up and wrote down his dreams and went back to sleep. In this way his body, which did not want to get up in the middle of the night, tried to fool him. However, the ruse only lasted a couple of nights. Then, one night while he was dreaming that he was awake and writing down his dream, he became sufficiently aware in his sleep to recognize what was going on. So he woke up and wrote down the dream that he was awake and writing down the dream. Within one week, he was writing down two, three, or four dreams every night.

Once you are able to awaken with your dreams, you can start to do other kinds of work in your sleep. For instance, you can actually study psychic subjects in your sleep.

Astral classes can best be explained as meetings at which your being studies methods of consciousness or psychic growth with other beings who are experts in these fields. Taking an astral class is a little bit like working with spirit guides.

You can either go into an astral class on purpose, or you can fall into one. If you start remembering dreams in which you are, for instance, attending lectures given by some prominent psychic teacher, or if you start remembering dreams in which friends or even unknown people are instructing you in healing, paying attention, etc., you have probably fallen into an astral class. Read your dream notebook periodically to get a sense of the direction your lessons are taking.

While we were writing this book, Bill fell into an astral class he found particularly exciting. Here is the dream:

> I'm with a group of people who are practicing, or learning, astral travel/levitation. The guide stands on one side of a metal contraption that looks like a vertical trapeze, and the student or initiate stands on the other. They go up together and the student flies.
>
> First a woman goes up. When she comes down, I say something—joking?—and the teacher, a tall woman with gray hair, holds out her hand to me. I'm scared. I stand before the contraption and I feel it start to work. I cry out and everything is "normal" again. Then I try once more and suddenly I'm flying.
>
> Time stands still for me, with regard to other people. The people in the room remain motionless, frozen in their positions. I have a bit of trouble navigating and realize it's because it's my first time, and that I'll learn to do it better. As if knowing that it will bring me down, I cry out again and fall—plummet?—for what seems a far, long distance, but which I see is no farther than the height of the room. Everyone is animated, and there are new people in the room.*

*The fact that there were new people in the room, and that everyone was animated again, seems to suggest that while time stood still for Bill, it did *not* stand still for the other people in the dream. This kind of disparity between time as *experienced by the self* on the astral plane and time as *observed for others* is remarkably similar to certain issues of relativity physics. For instance, when a star collapses and becomes a black hole, at some point in its collapse time stands still for the star as seen by observers here on Earth. For the star, however, time does not stand still, and it continues to collapse. Once again, there is a curious parallel between psychic experiences and the discovereis of advanced science, which seems to validate the experiences psychics have had for many centuries. These kinds of parallels are occurring with increasing frequency as science matures.

If you wish, you can attend an astral class intentionally. As with all forms of psychic work we've discussed in this book, what you do will look a lot like an exercise in imagination. However, in doing these exercises you may discover that there's more to imagination than meets the unimaginative eye.

To "enroll" in an astral class, determine what area or areas you want to "study." Go into trance after getting into bed and ask yourself who's teaching that class. Take the name or face that comes to your mind first. If it doesn't make sense to you—if Ben Franklin is giving a course on the energy body, or if your grandmother is teaching about the functions of creativity—that's perfectly okay. Some being who is a great teacher in the nonphysical realm may have come back this incarnation as your newsboy for the purpose of getting to know the people on his route. Keep track of your dreams and see what you learn.

Of course, you can work on your questions individually, too. After you have gone into trance and grounded yourself and begun to fall asleep, define what it is you want to work on, and tell yourself, "I want to know what I get out of —— ——," or "I want to confront my fear of ———," or "I want to know what ———means," or "I want to know what to do to cure———." If you don't have a satisfactory answer, or at least a lead, within a few nights, rephrase the question more clearly and precisely, or work on learning why you won't let yourself know what you want to know.

It will help you in doing this kind of dream work to get to know the ways in which your mind works. There are certain general symbols that seem to occur in virtually everyone's dreams, at least in a particular historical era or in a particular part of the world. In addition, everyone's specific system of symbology is unique, and you will have to learn what certain people, places, actions, or things mean to you. You can do this by looking for patterns and repeating symbols that crop up in your dreams, and simply asking yourself, while awake, what they mean—if their meanings are not already clear to you. Also, a symbol may not become clear right away; if you read over your dreams a few weeks or months after you have them, you'll begin to see ways in which they apply to your life that you might not have seen at first. What you learn will be applicable, in general terms, to the dreams you are having at the time you review your dreams, as well as later on.

Bill has done a fair amount of dream work over the past few years, and has observed both for himself and for others that in piecing together your own system of symbols, it helps to remember that the mind is a terrific punster. If you start dreaming about the bottoms of feet, consider that you may be dreaming about your soul (sole = soul). If you dream about a ruling king or queen, or if you dream about a bridled horse, you may also, on another level, be dreaming about water (reign = rein = rain), and it might be instructive, then, to find out what water means to you. The mind does not only pun in words; it also puns in pictures, sounds, sensations, etc. Any system of symbology you use on a conscious level, your mind will use in your dreams.

When Bill was looking for the solution to a specific problem a couple of years ago, he dreamed that he was in an underground garage, chasing a bull. As he ran after the bull, he kept dropping his key chain. When he took a look at his dream in the cold light of morning, interpreting it in terms of his own symbols, he saw that in the lower levels of his consciousness (underground), he kept losing the answer (dropping the "key") to his question because he was so busy chasing the bull (shit) in his life. On the basis of the dream information, he was able to spend a little less time chasing the bull and start to use the key to unlock his question.

182

Once you get familiar with dream work it quickly becomes apparent that your dream exchanges can go either way: You can receive information from your dreams, but you can also direct them. Of course, in theatrical terms you always direct them. You are the creator of your experience. Here, however, we are talking about a different kind of directing, one in which you consciously and intentionally determine the specific use to which you want to put your dreams.

The process of astral healing resembles a combination of dream work and absent healing. In a sense, it is a form of absent healing, and should be approached with the same caution and reserve. People have the right to have their illnesses, and it is bad psychic manners to fly around on the astral plane at night poking your healing fingers into people's psychic or physical sore spots.

As with any other absent healing, it is highly preferable not to procede without the permission of the person you intend to heal. If you have such permission, however, go to it.

1. After you get into bed, go into trance and ground yourself.

2. Clear your mind and create a mental picture of the person you are healing. As with a simple absent healing, if you don't know what the person looks like, create a silhouette or an undetailed picture of him as you imagine he looks.

3. Ground the person in your picture, and fill his body and aura with orange light.

4. If you're working on a particular part of the body, concentrate the orange strongly on that part.

5. Tell the person in your picture that you will meet with him shortly for the purpose of giving him a healing.

6. Go to sleep. Goodnight. Record any dreams you have tonight, and see if they pertain to the healing. When you speak with the person next, you might find out if he had any unusual dreams or waking sensations around the time you were working.

To conclude this chapter, let's take a quick look at an old nursery song. Pretend that your body is to your being what a boat is to your body as you float down the river of life, and imagine what would happen to the frantic strivings for fame, fortune, power, and position in the world if we began to take Mother Goose seriously. Now, everybody follow the bouncing ball:

> *Row, row, row your boat*
> *Gently down the stream.*
> *Merrily, merrily, merrily, merrily,*
> *Life is but a dream.*

# 8

## MORE ADVANCED HEALING AND READING TECHNIQUES

**How to Read Past Lives**

We have found that when many people become interested in psychic stuff, one of their first questions is, "Can you tell me about my past lives?"

Reading past lives sounds like a mystical and mysterious ability, but really it is no more difficult than any of the exercises in this book. Before we tell you how you can read your own and your friends' past lives, we will tell you a little more about what they are.

As we said earlier in this book, each being incarnates in a series of bodies. Each new body that it enters, or each new life that it takes, is the next step on its road of growth and development. This does not mean that a person becomes holier and holier with each life. A being may take a life as a very nasty person, because the next step in its growth is learning about nastiness. It is conventional to speak of sequential lives—that is, lives that take place one after another. It is our understanding, as well as the understanding of numerous physicists and mystics, that all time is simultaneous—that 2,000 B.C., today, and 2,000 A.D. all occur at once. Thus, all a being's lives may be seen as taking place "at the same time."

A being's choices about which bodies it will take are also governed by karma, which, as we have discussed, is a complex network of agreements and relationships with other beings. These relationships can range from very positive to very negative. When your rich aunt dies and unexpectedly leaves you a fabulous inheritance, it may be that you did her a favor in a past life, and this is her way of saying "thank you." Or when a mass murderer slaughters seemingly innocent victims, it may be that he felt deeply wronged by them in a past life. It is important to recognize, however, that people should make their decisions based on the experiences of *this* life. People *in* this life must live *with* this life. For example, one does not ignore the present-day crimes of a mass murderer because he had a particularly unhappy past life.

Of all the soil for psychic charlatanry, past life reading is the most fertile. Any psychic knows that he will win the hearts of his clients or friends by telling them that they were Egyptian princesses, noblemen on the lost continent of Atlantis, or Beethoven. Another way to woo and impress people is to tell them they were wicked or dangerous in their past lives and therefore are not responsible for their actions today. We have seen many people who could not have been happier to discover that they were black magicians or warlords. Others are happy to have been pillaged and robbed, burned at the stake as witches, or in any way martyred. Their past life troubles serve as convenient fodder for their belief that life has always been unjust to them and that it will, of necessity, go on being so.

Dealing with karma is principally a matter of being willing to handle the present moment. And Amy finds in her readings that if someone is committed to handling his or her problems in the here and now, an overview of karmic patterns and past lives can be instructive and interesting.

Sometimes it is helpful for someone to be told about a past life which was particularly happy for him. The memories of that life are stored in the being's memory, and talking about this past life can bring it into a person's consciousness. The deep memory of such happiness can be soul-satisfying to someone in a period of unhappiness, or it can remind him of his being's innate capacity for happiness. Or, it can remind him that in the long haul, his momentary problems are not so momentous.

Sometimes people are repeating the same karmic patterns over and over with little progress or resolution. In such a case, a past life reading can point out to the person the futility of playing the same miserable game forever.

Before giving someone a past life reading, ask yourself if he will use the information you give him wisely. There is no sense in giving someone more fuel for getting away from solving his current problems by taking him on a trip into the distant past.

A frequent question asked by curious past-lifers is, "Did I know my wife/husband/brother/mother/daughter/lover in a past life?" The answer is almost always "yes." Intimate relationships are usually karmic ones—your close friends and relations are almost always old friends. Another oft-asked question in Amy's experience is, "Has my recently deceased wife/husband/mother/father/etc., just reincarnated as my child?" The answer is usually "no." Most beings do not reincarnate so quickly, and most beings want to take a rest period between karmic cycles with a particular group of people.

Contrary to popular belief, most people have had a great many past lives, rather than just one or two. Therefore, if you sat down to read someone's past lives, it could take you days to read all of them.

We have found that the influence of our different lives on our present lives varies constantly. The lessons of one life as a pirate may be totally useless to you now, while your time as a Greek scholar may provide a wealth of unconscious information. Everything you have ever learned in your various lives is stored deep inside you. Although for most people this process is unconscious, the pictures or memories will appear in your aura in the form of images when you need to remember the lessons of a past life.

A clairvoyant, studying an aura for past life information, might witness a scene taking place, observe people in the dress of other ages, or even hear a conversation from ancient times. Or, he may see symbols in the aura representing a person's different lives—a lotus flower associated with a Buddhist life, or a life involving some form of meditation; a cross with a Christian life; a mandala with a life in India or Tibet; etc.

Someone who has become interested in Eastern philosophy or meditation may, without being aware of it, be drawing on what he has learned in a past life as an Easterner. It would not be surprising to see pictures from that part of the world floating in his aura. As he finishes psychically learning his Eastern lessons, the pictures will fade and recede from the aura, and new ones appear to take their place. A person's aura can sport scenes from one life or many at a time, in addition to pictures from unresolved issues in his or her present life.

Reading past lives is really very much like reading auras and chakras: The key is to relax, allow impressions to come to you, no matter how peculiar or unexpected, and follow your intuition. Practice in psychic reading will tell you when it is or is not a good idea to answer someone's questions about his past lives. You can use the Yes/No exercise to help you decide. For those times when you wish to read past lives, use the following exercise. Only do this exercise with someone you have read before, or who seems particularly comfortable with psychic reading. Past lives can be scary for a beginner. You may also adapt this exercise to read your own past lives.

1. Sit in the psychic posture.

2. Clear your mind, and focus on the question, "What are the past lives appearing in my friend's aura at this time?"

3. Now look at your friend's aura. Allow any impressions or pictures to come to you. Ask yourself for a general time and geographical location where these scenes are taking place.

4. Ask yourself if the past life from which the images come has any meaning or message for your friend in the present day. Notice if your intuition tells you that someone from your friend's present life has also appeared in this past life, and if so, in what capacity?

5. Dissolve these pictures. Come out of trance.

After this exercise, it is a particularly good time to make a joke or otherwise make your bodies real.

## Predictions, Precognition, and Future Lives

Can we see into the future? Can we predict our own futures, as well as those of others? People often ask such questions of psychics. As you begin to tap your psychic awareness, you probably wonder if these abilities are within your reach. If your friends are aware that you are using your psychic powers, they may well expect you to see into their futures.

As we see it, the future is a fluid, flexible thing. It is not set and sealed, defined and immutable, unchangeable and irrevocably destined. The future is *always* changing. Every moment of your life you are creating your future, from your smallest decisions to the largest.

When a psychic looks at your future, he or she is observing what you have planned for yourself at the *moment.* If his or her prediction does not come true, it is not necessarily because your psychic is a quack; it may be that you have changed your own plans, even without realizing it consciously. Or the psychic may be reading symbols accurately and interpreting them according to a system which differs from your own.

Several years ago, Bill spent the summer on the East Coast and went to see a psychic who had an excellent reputation among his friends. For the most part, Bill found her reading extremely accurate. Then she began to read his future. She saw him staying on in the East for two years before moving to a very different geographical environment. But he made no plans to stay East, and went back home to California when the summer was over. Well, he thought, she botched that one.

But as the two years passed, Bill found that his life was filled with the same sorts of concerns that had occupied his time during the summer in the East. And at the end of that period, he began to move into a different mental and emotional environment. The psychic had read his mental whereabouts accurately but had interpreted them in physical terms.

When you look at your own future, be it in meditation or dreams, you are observing some of the many possibilities you have set up for yourself.

We cannot tell you whether or not it is wise to exercise your precognitive abilities for yourself or for others. For some it is a blessing, for others a curse. As with any psychic ability, of course, you need not let *it* use *you.*

Some people with precognitive abilities tend to see only negative things, such as disasters, assassinations, etc. This is a choice which these people make, although they may feel that it is out of their control. Quite often people ask Amy, "Can you tell me when someone is going to die?" Her answer is, "I have consciously chosen *not* to be aware of someone's imminent death. I feel that it would be too great a responsibility for me and I would rather not know."

Lewis Bostwick once told Amy a story about Jeane Dixon, the famous precognitive psychic. She apparently called him in tears after John Kennedy's assassination, saying, "I tried and tried to reach the White House to warn him, but they wouldn't let me get through!" Lewis's answer to her was, "Well, Jeane, maybe you weren't supposed to."

There is a fine line between guidance and interfering with someone else's plan for his life. When Amy is asked to read someone's future, she is always cautious. She has made highly successful predictions, predictions that never came true, and has refused to predict at all. If her intuition tells her that it will help her client to look at possible trends and possible futures, and if she thinks he will understand

191

that these trends are subject to change, she will venture into it.

All too often, however, people are highly "programmable." If you say to them, "You will become a doctor/lawyer /Indian chief," they'll go right out and do just that. It is a convenient way to avoid responsibility for your own decisions to say, "Well, my psychic told me to do such and such."

If you feel that you can help people in this way, and you would like to see their futures, please remember to tell them that the ultimate decision always lies in their hands.

As you might have guessed by now, since there are past lives, there must be future lives as well. Indeed there are, and strange as it may seem, we are all planning our future lives right now, just as we are planning the futures of *this* life. It is possible to see future lives in the aura much as we have shown you to see past lives. However, we discourage this practice: It can be psychically confusing and distressing to see a future life.

## How to Read Your Future

Here are two exercises for reading your own future. You can use them to read someone else's future as well.

1. Sit in the psychic posture.

2. On your mental screen, draw three circles. Label one of them Six Months, one of them One Year, and the third one Five Years.

3. Think of three things you would like to have. They can be anything from a new car or house to quitting smoking,

losing weight, getting along with your boss, or whatever.

4. Postulate that your three desires will go into the different circles. Do not *place* the wishes into the circles, rather watch them go in. More than one thing can go into a circle. Watch what goes where, and notice how you feel about it. If you would like to make any changes in which wish went into what circle, move it from one circle to another. If something remains outside all three circles, ask that a number appear beneath it. This number is to tell you how many years it will be before you allow your desire to come to pass.

5. Dissolve the circles, and come out of trance.

## Reading Your Future Roses

1. Sit in the psychic posture.

2. On your mental screen, make a rose for yourself. Examine the rose. Notice what you like and dislike about it.

3. To the left of it make another rose. This is a rose for you six months ago. Notice the differences, if there are any, between the first and the second rose.

4. Make a third rose, on the right. This is a rose for you six months from now. If there is anything you don't like about this rose, be it color, shape, or size, change it. Dissolve all the roses.

5. Make another rose. This is a rose for you one year from now. Make another rose. This is a rose for you five years from now. Make as many more roses as you wish, for as many years. If you don't like them, change them into what you like. Dissolve all your roses, and come out of trance.

## How to Talk to Spirit Guides

In the second chapter of this book, we discussed spirit healing guides, those disembodied helpers who aid many healers in their work. We advised you not to work with such guides without the help of a trained psychic.

However, there is another type of guide with whom you may communicate without much difficulty or danger. Everyone has at least one "spirit guide" inhabiting the outer edges of his or her aura, part time.

As we have mentioned, when beings are not incarnated in a body, they have many duties and functions to fulfill on the astral plane. One or more may choose to take a part-time or full-time job as your spiritual advisor. It may come as a surprise to realize that you always have company, because most people never communicate *consciously* with their spirit guides at all. Most of the communication goes on on the astral plane, when you are asleep. Sometimes, people converse with themselves in different "little voices," talking over their problems, their decisions, etc., with themselves. If you find yourself doing this, you may be speaking with your "inner voice" (the voice of your *being*, not the voice of your *mind.*); but it may also be one of your guides, with whom you are having a clairaudient communication. We have often heard people say that they felt they had a guardian angel, or someone watching over them—they have sensed the presence of their guides.

When you decided to incarnate and be born, it was an auspicious event in the psychic community. A number of beings who were your friends on the astral plane, or acquaintances from past lives, attended this event. Of this spiritual assemblage in the hospital room, a few remained around you to see that you were in good health, that you

194

were properly reoriented to the physical plane, etc. They act as your companions and advisors. However, if it was your karma as a baby to be ill, your guides could not interfere with your plans, and this continues to be true throughout your life.

As you grew older, more guides entered into your sphere. By the time people are adults, they have an average of five or six guides. Often, one guide will be the most prominent, and each of the others will have its personal province. For example, one guide may concern itself with your work and career, another with your health, another with your spiritual development, another with your sexual relations, etc. Throughout your life, your guides come and go, as you change and your needs change. If you take on a new, important, and difficult task, you may have a guide specifically for the duration of that task. Other guides may remain with you for the better part of your lifetime

We are going to give you some exercises for getting in touch with your guides. It is important to mention once again what we said earlier about spirit healers: *Just because these are your out-of-body guides, their opinions are not always "right" for you.* Take their advice with a grain of salt, as you would that of your in-body advisors. They are here to aid you, not to run your life.

There are many different ways to communicate with your guides and with other people's. Amy sees guides in different ways at different times. Sometimes, when she looks in someone's aura for his guides, she sees what appear to be different-colored balls of light. Other times, she receives an image of a person. When a guide appears in a human form, it has chosen to present itself to you in the guise of one of its favorite lives, or one that might make you more comfortable talking to it.

Back in the days when Bill was first getting to know his guides, he became familiar with his principal guide, who usually appeared to him as a tall, broad old man in a kind of colorless robe, vaguely green and gray. He looked more like an enormous, lichen-covered rock than anything else. One day Bill asked his guide to appear in a form he would be more likely to recognize, and the guide showed up as a man about thirty years old from the American Colonial period, with a white ponytail wig, knee socks, and knickers. And Bill himself appeared behind the guide, in the form of a pudgy blonde woman. Apparently, some time in the latter half of the eighteenth century, Bill had been a woman, the mistress of the man who was, in this lifetime, his principal guide.

So, while a guide really does not have a sex or a nationality, you may see a plump Buddha, or an elegant Frenchwoman, or whatever. We know of one psychic whose guide appeared to him as a shapely blonde in hotpants. In some cultures, such as those of many American Indian tribes, the guides are traditionally seen in animal form.

1. Sit in the psychic posture for a moment, and then clasp your hands together. This creates a closed circuit of energy.

2. Form in your mind the request for one of your guides to appear to you.

3. Open your hands, thus creating a receptive posture, and let your impressions come to you. You may see a person, or you may see a pattern or a color. Or, you may not see anything—you may *know* what your guide looks like, or you may hear a voice describing him or her to you.

4. Ask your guide for a name. You may hear one, or see a name printed on your mental screen, or you may know it.

5. Ask your guide what his or her purpose is for you, or the special area of attention.

6. Say thank you and good-bye, and come out of trance.

You may repeat this process as many times as you wish, for your different guides. You may also request to see a certain guide simply by asking mentally, "I would like to see my health guide," or whatever.

The following exercise is for obtaining specific information and advice from your guides.

### Asking Your Guides for Guidance

1. Sit in the psychic posture, with your hands clasped. Form a question in your mind. This can be anything. "Should I take that new job?" "How can I better communicate with my boyfriend?" "Would that new diet I've been reading about really help me?" "Is that book about psychic healing I've been reading really hocus-pocus?" Clear your mind, and concentrate on your question.

2. Open your hands, placing them face up on your knees, and receive the answer. Hear it, know it, or see it in writing on your mental screen.

3. Say thank you and good-bye to your guides, and come out of trance. Make your body real.

In her readings, Amy often talks to her readee's guides for help and advice about her readee. Sometimes there is something they have been wishing to communicate to the person, and they ask Amy to tell him. Usually it is good advice, but she uses her discretion, sometimes telling the guides, "No, I'm sorry, but I don't think that information is appropriate."

To talk to another person's guides, use the same methods you used with your own guides in the previous two exercises. We have found that many people are interested in hearing about their guides, and you may find it fun to practice your psychic skills in this way.

## Out-of-Body Healing

Out-of-body healing is closely related to absent healing, which we discussed in Chapter 2. In absent healing, the healer directs his attention to the mental image of a person who is not present. In out-of-body healing, the healer's astral body actually steps out of his physical body and enters the aura of the person he is healing. Some healers are more comfortable with out-of-body work, others with absent healing. Some people find that their clairvoyant experience is heightened using this technique. We know of one medium who, when she leaves her body to do readings, takes advantage of her free time. She checks in on her husband at work and her children at home. In an experiment to test her out-of-body recall, she astrally read a book which was lying open in the room next to her. Returning to her body, she was able to relate the first paragraph verbatim and paraphrase the remaining two pages.

We have placed the section on out-of-body healing in the advanced chapter because it is not something to do casually. You must have a real sense of what it is to be *in* your body before you can go traipsing in and out. Another problem with this work is that you can easily leave your energy in the other person's aura if you are not careful.

This exercise begins with part of an exercise you did earlier, "Being in the Corner of the Room" (Chapter 3).

1. Sit in the psychic posture. Be sure you are well grounded. Choose a person to heal, following the suggestions given in Chapter 2 on absent healing.

2. Be in the corner of the room. Then return to the center of your head. Repeat this process three times.

3. Once more, be in the corner of the room. Next, be in some other room in your house or apartment. Does it feel different?

4. From here, be on the roof of your building.

5. Next, be on a cloud in the sky.

6. Then be in your friend's aura. What does it feel like? Can you see the colors of the aura? Ground your friend. Then clean his aura by bringing in cosmic energy and washing it over the aura.

7. Enter into your friend's first chakra. Clean it as you did the aura.

8. Go through the chakras, one by one, and clean them.

9. If there is a particular illness in a part of your friend's body, go to that area and imagine orange energy washing over it.

10. Be back in the center of your head.

11. Place a magnet in your aura and draw to it any of your energy that has been left in your friend's aura. Repeat the process in reverse.

12. Come out of trance.

### Acquainting Your Being with Your Body

1. Sit in the psychic posture. Run the color gold through your body.

2. Make a rose for yourself. Examine it fully—its color, its scent, its petals.

3. Where you usually put the sun in the picture, make

another rose. This is a rose for your being. Examine this rose.

4. Bring the second rose down and place it on top of the first rose, letting the two roses merge.

5. Dissolve the two roses, and come out of trance.

# 9

# COMIC CONSCIOUSNESS AND KARMIC RELIEF

## Zap! Now You're Psychic

As you approach this last chapter, you may be wondering, "Did I do it right?" "Am I really psychic?" No matter what you did, or how, you did it right. If you have far surpassed the expectations you had when you began this book, congratulations. If you are disappointed with your progress, have no fear. Merely by doing the exercises in this book, you have sparked wondrous creative forces within yourself. The results of this sparking may take months, even many years, to fully unfold.

We trust that what you've learned in this book will actually enable you to cure physical ailments, at least some of the time. Also, we trust that it will provide you with a richer experience of being alive and with greater pleasure in all your day-to-day activities.

As we've said, being a psychic healer, and using your psychic abilities, does not necessarily mean that your life will be a bed of thornless roses. Yet, you may find that by practicing some of the exercises in this book—such as grounding and running energy, and keeping your own aura and chakras in good, clean condition—the "bad" things in your life will seem to be not quite so bad as they used to, while the "good" things will seem better than before.

As we said in the first chapters of this book, you *are* psychic, and you *are* a psychic healer. This book has been a course in coming to recognize what was already present *in* your life, rather than a course in adding something *to* your life. The same holds true for your awareness. Your senses, for example, are always perceiving and taking in information for you: Your eyes always see, your ears always hear, your skin always feels, your nose always smells, your mouth always tastes. And your emotions are always aware: You always feel happy, or sad, or quiet, or excited, or neutral, or something. And your mind is always aware: It is always thinking, and it is always thinking about what it's thinking. Most of the time we don't pay attention to the processes of our own senses, or emotions, or intellects. But they are going on anyway; and being psychic is activating and working with those processes that are already going on.

We have said that being psychic is not "important," any more than being a doctor, or a writer, or an Indian chief is important. It is just a thing to be. There are many things to be, and one is no "better" than another. But living life as a psychic—knowing that you *are* psychic, and using your abilities in the smallest, day-to-day things you do—does seem to expand people's perceptions, expand their enthusiasm for living, and in general make life more enjoyable.

Using the psychic side of your life is invigorating, and in a sense it makes your world larger: There is always more to be psychic about, there is always more to examine and experience. Indeed, as far as we can tell there is no end to the game of life.

"Turning on" psychically will do many different things to different people. You may choose to actively pursue psychic or spiritual fields; you may find that things are changing in whatever areas of interest you already pursue; you may find yourself becoming interested in new creative areas, not specifically psychic; or you may find that your daily life relationships run a little more smoothly. Whatever happens for you, we would love to hear about it.

## Suggested Reading

There are many, many books about psychic phenomena and related "mysteries." The following list is made up of a few we have found especially valuable.

FRITJOF CAPRA,
> *The Tao of Physics*

CARLOS CASTANEDA
> *A Separate Reality*
> *The Teachings of Don Juan*
> *Journey to Ixtlan*
> *Tales of Power*

RAM DASS
> *Grist for the Mill*

ANN FARADAY
> *The Dream Game*

FRANCESCA FREEMANTLE AND CHÖGYAM
TRUNGPA (trans.)
*The Tibetan Book of the Dead*
LAMA GOVINDA
*The Way of the White Clouds*
G. I. GURDJIEFF
*Meetings with Remarkable Men*
ESTHER HARDING
*The Way of All Women*
EUGEN HERRIGEL
*Zen in the Art of Archery*
*The Method of Zen*
L. RON HUBBARD
*Dianetics*
ALDOUS HUXLEY
*The Perennial Philosophy*
RICHARD WILHELM (trans.)
*I Ching*
WILLIAM JAMES
*The Varieties of Religious Experience*
STANLEY KELEMAN
*Living Your Dying*
R. D. LAING
*The Politics of Experience*
*The Divided Self*
TIMOTHY LEARY
*Exo-psychology*
LAURENCE LESHAN
*The Medium, the Mystic, and the Physicist*
JOHN LILLY
*The Center of the Cyclone*
JEFFREY MISHLOVE
*The Roots of Consciousness*

ROBERT A. MONROE
*Journeys Out of the Body*
RAYMOND A. MOODY, M.D.
*Life After Life*
THELMA MOSS
*The Probability of the Impossible*
SHEILA OSTRANDER AND LYNN SCHROEDER
*Psychic Discoveries Behind the Iron Curtain*
P. D. OUSPENSKY
*In Search of the Miraculous*
BHAGWAN SHREE RAJNEESH
*The Book of the Secrets*
JANE ROBERTS
*The Seth Material*
*Seth Speaks*
*Adventures in Consciousness*
*The Nature of Personal Reality*
*Psychic Politics*
IDRIES SHAH
*The Sufis*
*The Exploits of the Incomparable Mulla Nasrudin*
DAVID ST. CLAIR
*Psychic Healers*
ALFRED STELTER
*Psi-Healing*
ALAN WATTS
*The Way of Zen*

Amy Wallace resides in Berkeley and has worked as a
professional psychic healer. She is the co-author of
THE PEOPLE'S ALMANAC, THE BOOK OF LISTS,
and THE INTIMATE SEX LIVES OF FAMOUS PEOPLE.

Bill Henkin resides in San Francisco and has been involved
with healing and psychic development for several years.
He has edited LIFE TIME, co-authored BY DESIGN and
THE JUKEBOX, and is the author of THE ROCKY HORROR PICTURE
SHOW BOOK.